The John and Ntombi Story

Jasper + Rosie. Dec. 2022

First published by The Grasped Image in 2022

ISBN 978-1-991220-15-8

Produced by Staging Post, a division of Jacana Media
Cover design by Sam van Straaten
Editing by Russell Martin
Proofreading by Lara Jacob
Set in Sabon LT Std 10.5/14.5pt
Printed and bound by ABC Press, Cape Town
Job no. 003958

The John and Ntombi Story

A MEMOIR OF THEIR LOVE AND TIMES

John Carneson

THE GRASPED IMAGE

www.thegraspedimage.com

Contents

Does the garraken flower open?
No, the daisy is the flower that opens
And do you open?
The daisy is the flower that opens

"Star Song of the Bushmen Women", adapted from *The Penguin Book of South African Verse*, edited by Jack Cope and Uys Krige (1960)

Acknowledgements

Ntombi, Gogo and our scattered families, for their stories, wit and wisdom.

Teachers, students and examiners of my master's course in creative writing at the University of the Witwatersrand.

My editor Linda Vergnani and the publishing and production team at Staging Post.

The author and publishers acknowledge permission to quote from the following writers: Bulent Karaalioglu ("Poor and Poor Villager"); Dennis Lee and Marie-Louise Gay (*Lizzy's Lion*, published by Fitzhenry and Whiteside, Leaside, Ontario, 1984).

Preface

NTOMBI AND I MET IN 1983 when we were in exile in Tanzania, and after a couple of years we moved with our infant daughter Busi to England. In 1993 we returned to Cape Town, just before the first democratic elections. Her mother Nomvula joined us shortly after the birth of our son Sipho, not having seen Ntombi for fourteen years. In the family we usually refer to her as Gogo, as she is the grandmother of our two children. She creates a quiet place that gives us a measure of stability and peace.

After retiring as a senior government official in 2018, I decided to write a memoir. I began with the first chapter, which is about accessing memories that in my case are normally obscured by stress. But where to go from there? I did not want to write a book about my achievements or my participation in the struggle.

My wife suggested I write a book about Gogo. Ntombi, a retired lieutenant colonel, is persuasive, and I thought it a good idea to tell the story of Gogo's life. It demands to be told, and Ntombi promised to assist as I hardly speak any isiZulu. Ntombi avoided my attempts to conduct formal research and began to tell anecdotes about her and her mother's shared history at dinner.

I vaguely wondered why she had begun insisting we have dinner together, which did not happen often after our children left home. I made sure there was a notebook and pen next to my plate when I set the table, and she insisted that I should sit next to her.

Being half deaf, I made no objections. When we finished eating, Ntombi would begin telling stories. Most often they were about her impoverished childhood, which she spent with Gogo until she was twelve years old.

Ntombi is wide and has a pinned-together spine and two artificial knees. She occupies a solid wooden armchair at the head of the table, where she can sit down and leave easily, and from where she can be queen, chairperson and operations manager. It also allowed her to tell the stories dramatically. The upper part of her body is strong, and she talked as much with her hands as her mouth. Warnings were given if I interrupted or contradicted her, with occasional physical and verbal threats when I became too irritating.

I realised that Ntombi had meant all along that I should write a book about her and include Gogo and me. Her tactic was to employ a form of respectful isiZulu speech called *hlonipha*. Alternatively, she was being devious, or both. I was never sure, which is probably the point of *hlonipha*.

Ntombi translated parts of her story for Gogo, who understands and speaks quite a lot of English. When the story involved Gogo, she would comment or add something in isiZulu or English. In a few hours I learned more about Ntombi's early life with Gogo than in the thirty-five years we have lived together.

It gradually dawned on me that the book would be about a struggle after all – the never-ending struggle between me and Ntombi. And it must be about love. Our stormy relationship revolves around our unbounded love for each other.

Early on in the writing process, after we had a violent argument, I asked Ntombi what would happen to the work if we parted for some reason. My words made her face twist up in a way that shocked me. "That will never happen," she replied. "You irritate me a lot, but you are now part of me." I silently vowed that only death would part us, and perhaps not even then.

The twenty chapters in the book cover three distinct periods: before we met, our lives together in exile, and our return to our homeland. This is reflected in the three sets of photographs. Each chapter is held together by themes or ideas, and may jump back and forth and roam around the untidy spaces inside my head.

Knowing my habits of wondering and wandering, I realised I needed expert help for the project to succeed. I therefore wrote the book as a thesis to be submitted for an MA in creative writing. The students critiqued one another, and my tutor kept me in check. Her ultimate weapon was you, good reader, when she told me that unless I removed irrelevant vignettes, you would get lost in the woods and never forgive me. I sneaked up and murdered many hilarious and interesting anecdotes, and tearfully agreed it was for the best.

My parents were veterans of the struggle against colonialism and its most extreme form, apartheid. The state tried to crush them and targeted their children as well. Ntombi's family also played an active part in the struggle in which she and other black people suffered injustice so terrible that the United Nations declared apartheid a crime against humanity.

While these are threads that are woven into our lives and appear in our story, the book is essentially about the two of us, and Gogo. This means revealing our different characters, and how we survived each other and the troubled times we lived through. We had to deal with the society we were born into, and then there was exile, the Cold War, and the realities of post-apartheid South Africa.

As we get older and grouchier, we become less tolerant of each other's perceived and actual faults and notions. Even I find my character annoying, and Ntombi every day confirms that I irritate her. I try to compensate with self-deprecatory humour, which helps me to survive and further annoys Ntombi. My life is often tough because of my many flaws, which Ntombi exposes by stripping away my excuses like a nurse removing sticking plasters.

It may seem strange that our relationship grows more tender and loving as we find each other in retirement, given our fights about South Africa and the rest of the planet. For decades, the African

National Congress (ANC) was a liberation movement we would have died to protect. One of the things we agree on is that it is now hopelessly dependent on networks of patronage and corruption and is beyond any kind of salvation.

What might start an argument could be a power cut or a revelation from the Commission of Enquiry on State Capture. Both are events that Ntombi says are linked to faction fighting within the ANC. I say a gang of criminals, parading as politicians, captured the ANC and much of the state.

Ntombi and I may have similar core values, but we are emotional and opinionated and see the world in different ways. I argue in the book that she is a peasant, a class I respect greatly. "That is me," she said, embracing the term. I think that is why she is strongly family oriented and takes things personally. I am middle class and, what is worse, I believe my views are more objective because I look at reality through the lenses of shaky theories and worn-out books. Ntombi often proves me wrong, but not all the time.

In our battles we reach for every weapon imaginable: bullets of racism, sexism and classism, bombs of fake news or half-truths, and bayonets made of personal grievances. But in the end we always find each other and make peace or declare a truce. Then we more or less agree on what must be done.

My conclusion is that the book is mostly about our love surviving and thriving despite difficult circumstances and large differences of background, beliefs and character. And it is about how an annoying white man and two strong Zulu women try to enrich their lives and enjoy old age together. Hopefully readers will find something in that mix that amuses or interests them or may even be of use.

One
I grind my bones

Vignette [vin'yet]
Noun: a brief evocative description, account, or episode.
Verb: portray (someone) in the style of a vignette; or to vignette someone.

IT WAS A WEEKDAY in January 2019, at around five in the afternoon, the time when I used to phone Ntombi to tell her I was working late. Instead, being retired, I was seated in the garden and I was feeling as fresh as if I had risen at dawn to edit a policy document. When I closed my eyes and snuffed the air, the feeling was explained. The cacophony of the inner city was gone and the air was relatively fresh.

I hardly knew our garden, lovingly evolved by Ntombi, its demigod. Yet there I was, sitting beside our swimming pool, arthritic fingers about to create a clutch of vignettes on paper.

Our bedroom has glass doors that lead onto the brick patio around the pool. I was sitting on the opposite side, at a garden table of plaited iron strips, under a bright green galvanised roof, high enough to give me a view of a pearly sky tinged with orange. I had come home from work one day and discovered Ntombi had hired a former army colleague and his sons to build this structure over the area. She loves low-maintenance people, structures and plants.

I could see somebody moving behind the lace curtains of our children's rooms. First the face appeared in Busi's room, and then in Sipho's, which was next to our bedroom. It was Nomvula Mbele, the mother of Ntombi, known as Gogo, who joined us when we returned from exile in 1993. The children have left home, but wherever they are, they will always be close to their Gogo and protective of her.

The pain in my hands distracted me, so I wrote a complaining poem, in the manner of a fictional bear who composed little complaining songs. I used to sing them to Busi. For instance, in painful pursuit of honey, the bear sang how nice it would be to be a bee. To distract myself further, I imagined I was a cranky old poet, plagued by imagined ex-wives, each one gaunter and more vengeful than her predecessor. I scribbled a poem on a paper napkin and then typed it.

Dearest dears the arthritic poet said
I grind my bones to make your bread

I could not be referring to Ntombi. She is my one and only wife and is not at all gaunt. She is the maker of bread although badly afflicted by degeneration of the joints, and her bones grind together worse than mine. Another couplet popped into my mind.

She's a mover, a shaker
A planter and a baker

Our house is somewhere near the centre of South Africa. At the bottom of the pool there is a plastic image of a compass, with the four cardinal points correctly aligned. Swimming through the stratosphere in directions suggested by the compass, I tried to catch glimpses of my past, which was covered by clouds of stress. I always suspected this was the result of my existence irritating the universe and Ntombi.

I swam to five places in Africa that I would reach if I travelled north, south, east and west. They were all places that surfaced as I flew through my memories, stirring up the sediments.

The first place was Tanzania, which I would reach if I flew north-east, using the updrafts as I approached the tropics. I fell from the sky, into a seat in a bus on its way to a game park forty kilometres from our home in Morogoro. The ANC had established an education complex outside the town, the Solomon Mahlangu Freedom College (SOMAFCO). Ntombi was seated next to me, surrounded by students, some of whom were from my history and English classes. We had fallen in love shortly after she arrived in Mazimbu to set up modern kitchens at the school.

We were going on one of our rare outings. Ntombi had never been to a game reserve before. Under apartheid such facilities were reserved for whites only. Her first remark after we entered the gate was, "The management is useless. Look how dirty those elephants are." I did not attempt to explain why they were so muddy.

After lunch at the lodge we walked back to the bus with the students. I asked her about a strange sound that kept repeating. "Is that a bird call or an insect?" Ntombi was surprised at my ignorance, "That is the knives and spoons some students have hidden in their socks," she explained.

My next flight of fancy was due north, to Zambia. In the 1980s, I stayed for two nights in Andrew's Motel in Lusaka. I was there to ask the United Nations Institute for Namibia – an educational body for Namibian exiles – to validate SOMAFCO exam results.

The ANC had booked five adjoining rooms at the motel. Someone told me that in the room next to mine was a young white South African security policewoman, who claimed she had deserted to the liberation movement. She shared the small room with an ANC soldier, a little older, who was guarding her. His hatred was palpable and her dislike of him was just as intense. The only way they could communicate was through ferocious games of chess. A tattered booklet on chess strategy by a Soviet grandmaster lay on the table between them.

The slightly built young woman seemed very naive and would not respond to any of my remarks that were remotely political, telling me instead that she was a highly trained policewoman. "I can run ten kilometres, right now, with a full pack," she said.

Thirty years later, I learned that by that time she was already a successful spy who had infiltrated anti-apartheid groups at her university, leading to the arrest of students and other activists. She had been trained by Craig Williamson, a notorious apartheid spy, who was her handler and had killed the mother and child of a close friend of my father. Her best friend at university, Bridget Hilton-Barber, was jailed because of her betrayal, and later wrote that they had thought her sympathetic to their cause.[1] I suspect now that she felt I was not worth the effort of putting on her radical act.

Having completed my work, I was on the way to the airport when someone from ANC intelligence approached and asked me what I thought of the young woman. I hesitated. Would my answer contribute to her being taken to Angola, and perhaps tortured and shot? I was not involved in that side of the struggle, but I thought it was unlikely, despite the horrors inflicted on us by the regime. My father had been tortured, and my sister of fourteen had been betrayed by an agent she thought was her friend and had slashed her wrists.

My guess was that the regime thought it could not lose. If the ANC trusted her, then she would be able to send information back to Pretoria. If she were killed or detained, perhaps they would put out stories of torture and rape to counter the growing international anti-apartheid movement.

I said, "She has not an atom of concern for black people or a shred of feeling for the struggle. My view is there is no way she could be genuine, having talked with her."

A few years ago, I learned that her name was Olivia Forsyth, when she was interviewed on South African radio, having written a book about her adventures. According to my Google research, the

ANC used her for a time, but the question then remained: whose agent was she? Finally, the head of ANC security detained her in Quatro, their prison camp in Angola. Others had her released and they kept her in a safe house in Luanda, from where she escaped to the British embassy. Thatcher's government, an ally of the apartheid state, put pressure on the Angolan government to allow her to return to South Africa, where apartheid security chiefs paraded her and praised her for being a heroine and their top agent.

If I swim a thousand kilometres south, descending over the scrubby Karoo through the mist to sea level, I could perch on the flat top of the mountain looking down on Cape Town. I was born there in 1951, in a hospital high up on the slopes of Table Mountain. It is now a hospice, and it seems right for me to complete the circle and die there. I would be visited by my sisters, Ruth and Lynn, who live on opposite sides of False Bay, which is formed by the crooking of the finger of land. Cape Town sits on the knuckle of the peninsula, like a jewel on a ring.

Both of my sisters have published books about themselves and our family. My younger sister Ruth wrote her memoir, *Girl on the Edge* (2014) and Lynn wrote *Red in the Rainbow* (2010) about our parents Fred and Sarah. I could never find the courage to write about our past, and so used the alchemy of fiction to transmute my fragmented memories into short stories which I shared with family and friends. It took me months to force myself to read my sisters' books. A single word might bring back memories that I had suppressed.

One such word was "ban". The banning of people by the apartheid government was intended to erase them from society. Fred Carneson, my father, was banned from writing, speaking in public, being quoted, entering a school, college or printers, or being in any kind of social gathering. He was forbidden to leave the magisterial district of Cape Town and had to report to the police weekly. He was also banned from talking to other people who themselves were "banned or listed or named", such as Sarah, my mother, who was all three things. A merciful magistrate gave them special permission to communicate with each other.

I have a street trader's badge somewhere that my father wore while selling door to door. He had been an editor of an opposition paper, *New Age*, which was banned. Anyone who offered Fred a job was visited by the security police. Hanging by my desk is one of the artworks he sold on commission, a fine pewter relief of a woman.

When I was a child, my parents explained little about what was going on. This was to protect me and them, but it generated waves of anxiety in me.

When in prison, sentenced for having banned books and for furthering the ends of banned organisations, my father, like all political prisoners, was banned from reading news in any form. After he was released, and for the rest of his life, he read several papers a day, sometimes driving around to chase the latest edition. He never quite survived torture and his eyes remained sad.

Political prisoners were isolated from other prisoners to keep them from news, among other reasons. My father told me that when they accidentally discovered that a man had walked on the moon, the prisoners made spaceship and moon hats and held a party.

One of my handful of poems was written about things I saw on the corner at the end of our street in Cape Town, where there was more life because of passing traffic and a small café. Such cafés were almost always owned by a Portuguese or Greek family. Even as a child, our "whites-only" streets felt empty and sterile, and the horrors of apartheid were kept at a distance. The only black people you saw were servants, who were not allowed any visitors.

From the café I once saw a double act of violence. I was perhaps nine. A tall black man appeared on the other side of the road, together with a woman. I was startled. It was rare to see a black couple, given the strict laws dictating where black people could move, work or stay. Then I saw him slide to the ground without a sound as she walked away holding a bread knife. There was a brilliant streak of blood on the high white wall. The exclusive nursing home behind the wall called an ambulance. It was a whites-only ambulance that came and then drove away, leaving him to quietly die alongside the gutter – an act of violence that shocked me more than the stabbing.

On another occasion, while I was buying my weekly comic, the *Beano*, and a Coke at the café, a scarred, shaven black man in tattered khaki marched into the shop. He asked for a loaf and a tin of condensed milk.

I had a nightmare that night, and forty years later I remembered the incident and the dream, and wrote a poem that I titled "Corner Shop".

As a child in a whites-only
And classier part of town
Buying a comic and Coke
I saw a black jailbird fly
Up the hill and into the shop
Buy a loaf and a small tin of condensed milk
Tear out and swallow the heart of the bread
Fill the loaf with the sweet sweet sticky milk
And wolf all of it down right there in the shop
Without losing the tiniest drop

That night I dreamed that the man,
Cooked up our world in a frying pan
He ate all the prison, the city and me
Then tipped all our bones into the sea

If I plunged into the bank of clouds I saw rolling in from the east, I could swim a thousand kilometres towards the town of Inhambane in Mozambique. I taught English there for two years after Mozambique liberated itself from Portuguese colonialism.

When unpacking some old boxes in my garage, I found a collection of photos from my time in Mozambique that capture some of its spirit. One is of a May Day festival with a graceful dancer wearing the horns of an antelope. Under colonial rule, anyone practising African culture, language or religion was classified as an indigene, without rights and subject to forced labour. Another picture shows a small boy standing straight on a podium. He is delivering a speech to bright, uplifted faces that are full of pride and hope.

While in Mozambique, I visited a Frelimo party school and met ten or so young men and women in a classroom. Someone dropped a pile of tin plates in the corridor outside. In less than fifteen seconds all of them had dived in turn through the open window and headed for the bush. This was the only way they could survive the Portuguese bombing of the schools and clinics built by Frelimo in liberated zones. I still have a picture given to me by a teacher at the school where I taught, showing the planes and children lying around with their limbs blown off.

Participating in the birth of a new society was perhaps the most valuable and profound experience of my life.

Soon after I arrived, I met an Italian health volunteer, who came from a nearby village where a young Mozambican woman had talked for an hour to a group of elders. She used a poster to show how malaria infects people. In that hour, three revolutions took place. No woman had ever lectured the elders, and the concept of a woman having the right to do so was revolutionary. They had never looked at a piece of paper before or interpreted its symbols and messages – the concept of printed pictures and writing giving them access to knowledge was revolutionary. Not one of them was literate. They were introduced to the scientific revolution by learning that the diseases ravaging their people could have natural causes and be prevented.

The apartheid regime, aided by Britain and America, began a new war through arming Renamo, an ethnically based guerrilla force established by the former Rhodesian security services and redeployed back to Mozambique. Their predations became worse after I left Mozambique, and a communal village I visited and photographed was attacked. More than two hundred women, children and old men were slaughtered, and the surviving children were forced to become soldiers.

Mozambique has not known a year of peace since it gained political independence. It has developed rapidly in some places and little in others. As in most post-colonial societies, many of the former liberators evolved into a greedy and corrupt elite, unable to defend their sovereignty and dreams from powerful predators. A new struggle emerges, and people like me, now aged and comfortable, must meet the eyes of the people, staring at us from our screens, and try to make the right decisions.

Heading west towards the sinking sun, I swam a thousand kilometres through the clear air, looking down on arid wastelands, until I saw the great rolling swells of the Atlantic. I landed near Port Nolloth, close to the mouth of the Orange River, where I once spent ten days at the home of a boy who went to school in Cape Town and stayed in our boarding house. We were hardly in our teens. I cannot remember how I got there – perhaps by ship.

At sunset on my first day, we joined a group of children who were following a tallish boy onto a beach. He was carrying an airgun that shot small lead pellets. Tiny striped mice were darting in and out of the shadows. Up went the gun and there was a crack as he pulled the trigger, and the spring was released. A mouse, perhaps five metres away, was knocked over and lay still. With one movement the boy reloaded and fired. He did not pause to breathe or take aim. Within a couple of minutes, a dozen mice lay dead.

For years after the incident, I tried to reach that standard of shooting with my own airgun and always paused for a split second and failed. I gave up only when I read that great shootists were found to have slower-than-average heartbeats.

My hands now struggle to hold a computer mouse, let alone a gun. My first conclusion is: arthritis is mightier than the pen and the sword. My second conclusion is that, after you retire, imagine taking off into the sunset. The mountains of problems seem small, so far below, and you may catch glimpses of places that were once hidden under clouds of care and worry.

Two
The bomb and the ghazal

Igama lamakhosikazi Malibongwe
Malibongwe Malibongwe igama lamakhosikazi Malibongwe
[The name of women be praised
Praise praise the name of women]
– Freedom song (isiZulu)[2]

THE NINTH OF AUGUST is the day of remembering that I found myself on earth, in apartheid Cape Town, sixty-nine years before. After being downloaded through a wetware portal belonging to my mother, I was duly classified white and ready for programming in a whites-only school.

An employee of the former apartheid Department of Home Affairs described to me the ritual examination as it was when she worked there. The worried parent handed over the baby, who was taken into the staffroom by two officials. The door was locked, and the baby was stripped and examined for racial indicators against a list. She told me that if there was any ambiguity or suspicion about an infant's race, "the real race experts from the Department of Social Development were called in". From then until now, she said quietly, it troubles my mind to think of what we did.

Happily, when I was five years old in 1956, an inspiring event happened on my birthday: the march of ten to twenty thousand female delegates, mostly poor and black, to present a petition against the extension of the pass laws to women. They confronted the might of the apartheid state, seating themselves outside the Union Buildings in Pretoria. The event is now commemorated as Women's Day, a national holiday. So, thanks to those women, I do not have to go to work on my birthday and can eat, drink and be as merry as a man can be.

The singing of the massed women shook the Union Buildings as they sang to Prime Minister Strijdom in isiZulu: "You have touched the women and dislodged a grinding stone, it will crush you." Indeed, he died within two years of the event. On my birthday this story is always told, and I am reminded to be respectful of my wife Ntombi and all women.

My mother Sarah Carneson could not attend the march as she was banned from all public meetings, but she told me about another delegation she had been part of that presented a petition to a previous prime minister in his office. It was after the war, and only white women were allowed in. The women were protesting against inflation and mass starvation. My mother was small and young and the last to leave, and as she did so, Jan Smuts patted her head and said, "There, there my girl, it will all come right."

In the 1950s and 1960s, South Africa was deliberately isolated from the world. Television was not allowed so that we could not be contaminated by news of nations freeing themselves from colonial bondage. We were, however, fed carefully crafted stories about nuns being raped and killed in the Congo and by the so-called Mau Mau in Kenya. As a young child hearing this propaganda, I was always puzzled by exactly what rape was and why nuns were involved.

In 1945, on the date that was my birthday, the United States dropped a second atomic bomb on Japan, rubbing away part of the city of Nagasaki in a few seconds. They had destroyed the city of Hiroshima a few days earlier.

Thoughts of the dropping of the Bomb do nibble at the joy of having a birthday on 9 August. As a child I played our small collection of vinyl records many thousands of times. I found out about the atomic bombing of Japan through a song by Pete Seeger. It was based on a poem by the Turkish poet Nazim Hikmet about Hiroshima. I still recall some lines:

> I come and stand by every door
> but none can hear my silent tread
> I am only seven, now as then, for I am dead, for I am dead.

News of the Cuban missile crisis seeped into my consciousness and created a vague fear, and when I left for England in 1966, I encountered a growing Ban the Bomb movement. A horror of nuclear war and fear of extinction became embedded in my mind.

This is one of my hidden Jungian complexes that I have recently started sharing with Ntombi to ease the burden, and she does likewise with hers. It is one of the joys of being retired together. I visualise these complexes as impossibly tangled knots, tied to every other one on earth by psychic threads because of our shared history as human beings. I call it Mad John's string theory. Perhaps I should employ a costly psychologist to hack my strings about with a psychic sword.

In 2016 I visited relatives who live in New York, for two weeks. It was just before Christmas and a week before Trump was elected. While I was mingling with the cold but merry international mob in the streets of Manhattan, a Trump quotation appeared on the side of buildings and he announced he was willing to use the Bomb. He gave a whole new meaning to New York being a melting pot, and I felt unsafe and threatened. The next morning I had the urge to write a poem, and the outline of a ghazal emerged.

Draft poems appear in my mind perhaps once a year and may take years to get right. The ghazal is a tricky poetic form which insists on each verse being unrelated to the others, with all verses except the last repeating the same word or phrase. Traditionally the last verse should refer ironically to the pen name of the author, which in my case is (in Afrikaans and isiZulu) Jan Mbali, or John the Writer.

Poetry works for me on a subconscious level, and the connection of the Bomb and my birth date may explain why in 2020, as I was turning sixty-nine, I decided to finish the ghazal. I was sitting in an office that Ntombi had created for me in the corner of our bedroom, a nest within a nest, and produced the following:

The Light and Dark Ghazal

The marmalade man promises himself a war.
It will go light, then forever go dark. Just as

A girl in a moving canoe dips her head like
a bird. She trails her hair in the dark water.

A boy strumming his guitar feels the vibration
of a universe that plays him. He sings dark songs.

Blind Georgina strokes a line of Blake and she says
everything that lives is holy. She smiles in the dark.

Two business women look at a contract and
say what a sweet deal. Their dark eyes shine.

I, Jan Mbali, gaze at a tree whose limbs
remind me of love. I think of my Ntombi.

When I read the poem, I saw it had the traditional themes of love and death. My main concern was how Ntombi would react to the use of her name and limbs. Wine is also traditional in the ghazal, but it was missing from the poem, perhaps because wine, of the spiritual or intoxicating kind, reminds me painfully of my gout, whose bite is sharper than a serpent's tooth. Ntombi would appreciate the absence of alcohol, as she became teetotal after downing a bottle of sherry at our wedding in London in the 1980s. Amazingly, it had no apparent effect or after-effect on her.

I used Ntombi's name at my peril, as she is a very discreet person when it comes to love. The only exception was when she was an officer and from time to time lectured young soldiers on its perils. She managed the military hospital kitchens, among other things, and whatever she warned them about – booze or sex or smoking – she said the impacted organ looked like fried liver. She once told her staff that if a man harassed her, she would kick his balls to mayonnaise.

That day, Ntombi was being birthday-boy nice to me and was lying down with the TV turned low, typing quietly on her smartphone. Earlier, Ntombi and I had listened to the poetry of Maya Angelou on the radio. I was delighted that Ntombi liked afternoon radio dramas and book readings, and then silently accused myself of being a racist, classist, sexist pig for being surprised. I knew that my guilt would nag at me as if it were a Jewish or Greek or any other kind of mother.

I explained that I had written a poem that mentioned her. Then I printed "Light and Dark Ghazal" and went to lie down and read it to her. She continued to type on her phone and look now and then at the TV. She also glanced at the poem.

The claws of the she-leopard remained sheathed, and my timid and trembling ghazal is still safe – for now.

That night, I forced myself to look at my conception in historical perspective. Of course, I had long known I was the biological product of Fred, a Catholic boy, and Sarah, a Jewish girl.

During World War II my parents fell in love after they arranged to meet at a hockey match my father was playing in. Fred was on leave from the army, and Sarah worked in a leftist book club that was part of a devilish Communist conspiracy. She used literature to ensnare innocent young intellectuals, soldiers and workers – among them my father.

Sarah promised to send him some radical literature, pamphlets that throbbed with evil in rhythm with her heart. Every line of type writhed suggestively, set by typesetters who were all members of the Communist-led trade unions.

When they learned to type, both Fred and Sarah had to repeat over and over, "Now is the time for all good men to join the party." It was included in the practice texts from the first manual for typists published in the nineteenth century. I assume there was also one about a quick brown fox jumping over a lazy dog that was clearly planted by anti-fox-hunting activists.

A rational being may conclude that the sentences were devised because they cover all the keys in a way useful for training. And the party referred to may have been an all-night Victorian rave that the author of the typing manual attended.

Creative historians allied to the Marmalade Man claim in their tweets and blogs that the phrase about joining the party never was in that famous typing manual, and that evil Commies invented the idea and cunningly inserted it in later manuals. It makes perfect sense to me, and clearly played a part in my parents' courtship.

My older sister Lynn disputes this, our mother having admitted that she ensnared our father with poetry. She fired Walt Whitman at him, then Rabindranath Tagore, and bombarded him with Omar Khayyam. (Two Commies and an Ay-rab, the Marmalade Man would comment.) What defeated the young soldier in 1940 was Li Po, the eighth-century Chinese poet. Telling of war, loneliness and love, a young soldier wrote:

My ruins of the heart,
Thoughts of you unending.

Well, it worked for them, and here I am.

The morning after my birthday was very John Keats-like, a fellow whose letters and poetry I had to study for my A-levels while in exile in England.

It was early spring, but it felt like Keats's poem "Ode to Autumn", which begins with "Season of mists and mellow fruitfulness", because Ntombi had begun pruning her vines and some fruit trees.

The feeling reminded me that whenever I seriously consider topping myself, as they called it in the 1960s – season of drugs and rock stars who topped themselves – I start repeating a line of Keats endlessly, "I am half in love with easeful death". Usually, I am being killed by a problem of my own making, which really twists a knife in your guts. It is often a problem for which Ntombi is justly punishing me: like falling for a crooked builder's tricks, losing half our savings, or wrecking the house she had lovingly improved.

Then something snaps and I shout, "I am now so stressed that the bloody situation is hilarious." I mutter variations on Keats to myself as I march round and round the swimming pool, "My balls ache and a drowsy numbness pains my sense as if some hemlock I have drunk" and sometimes "My mind aches and..." or "My conscience aches...", and so on. Then I grin like Yorick's skull and see a way out of whatever grave I have dug and fallen into.

Well, it works for me.

Three

Uncovering my parents, Fred and Sarah

Sarah Carneson was very small with a smile and laugh that quickly evaporated as she uttered very serious thoughts, her brightness undiminished by her recent release from detention with Dora under the 1960 State of Emergency.
– Stephanie Kemp, *My Life*, 2017

THERE ARE MANY REASONS why I know relatively little about my roots in terms of the families and childhoods of my parents. I had little contact with my mother's family and almost no contact with my father's, for reasons of persecution, ideology, class and geography.

When I was a child, our family was targeted by the white apartheid state, which was locked into a total war against the just demands of ninety per cent of the population. These were the black people, who were classified as non-white and non-citizens. My parents were among the small number of whites who dedicated their lives to establishing a non-racial, democratic society.

Fred had to leave secondary school at fourteen, although he was the first in his family to get beyond elementary school. With some exceptions, the white working-class family he came from was largely pro-government and was based in Natal. My mother Sarah came from a middle-class Jewish family who had settled in Johannesburg. They had anti-colonial and socialist roots, but by the 1940s the majority conformed to the dominant values of white society. Later, many of those who did not left South Africa.

We lived in Cape Town, more than a thousand kilometres from either Fred's or Sarah's families. As activists, my parents were banned from travelling beyond a few suburbs of Cape Town and had to report to the police weekly. When the struggle against apartheid intensified, the reaction of the authorities became increasingly brutal. Even sympathetic white families avoided us. A pervasive fear was generated by oppressive laws and the actions of the powerful security establishment. Comrades of my parents like "Looksmart" Ngudle and Vuyisile Mini were tortured to death or executed. Our house was regularly raided and searched in the early hours, while I hid under the blankets, deeply ashamed of being afraid and helpless. The trauma and shame have persisted and still stay with me.

There was a strong chance that things said in Mount Pleasant, the guest house that was also our home, would be recorded by the security police. It was a grand old house with wooden shutters, bought for my parents by my Russian-Jewish grandmother. We occupied most of the rooms on the ground floor, and guests the upper floor. Casual chats about my parents' wartime experiences, for example, would create risks for whoever was mentioned. We once came across a microphone dangling down a chimney, and I found a tracking device under our car.

An elderly, devout Afrikaner couple who rented a large room upstairs were put under immense pressure to spy on us and quietly told my father they had refused. I will never forget seeing them on their knees praying in front of a window, with light streaming onto their serene faces.

Throughout this period, Fred and Sarah remained active in the clandestine movements opposed to apartheid, and so were careful not to share any sensitive information with me. I did now and again carry messages to comrades who lived nearby, locked down by similar banning orders.

My parents were non-believers, so it was not surprising that when I first went to school at the age of five, I was confused about my ethnicity and religious affiliations. For several years teachers and family members would tease me about two things that happened on my first day. I went to school for the first time with my shorts on back-to-front, and, when asked what religion I was, I answered that I did not know.

Even my name, John, was confusing, as Jews considered me to be a Jew by matrilineal descent, my mother having being born Sarah Rubin. She told me they picked John because they thought it a manly name. This never saved me from being the target of anti-Semitic attacks, perhaps in part because I was a small child, and I am neither tall nor broad. Being atheists, they should not have tempted God. I would have settled for being called Aaron, for then I would have been first on any list and would probably have been born a strong, thickset, hairy Jew, of whom there were many in the struggle.

At least three young white men I knew as a child committed suicide. The moral and political wasteland of the 1960s distressed them unbearably, although I think only one was a political activist. His name was Evan, an Afrikaner university student, who was deputy scoutmaster of the pack I belonged to.

Evan was arrested at an anti-racist demonstration. His wealthy father encouraged the court to be harsh, and he was sentenced to be flogged. I doubt the physical trauma was the cause of his suicide. He was as strong as an ox. I was among the boy scouts who conspired to put two bricks in his rucksack before he climbed up Table Mountain. He never noticed.

When I finally had a chance to talk to my parents about their past, my father was in his late seventies and was still wary about disclosing too much, even though we were living in the new South Africa. He died when he was eighty, and my mother was then eighty-four. When she was in her nineties, her memories began to fade and became a little confused. I have had to add to my knowledge of their past from what I can learn from books or any other source.

Recently I was given a glimpse into this past when Stephanie Kemp, who became a political activist and worked for the African Resistance Movement in the 1960s, spoke at the relaunch of her autobiography. Coming from a conservative Afrikaner family in a small town, she talked about meeting my mother while a student in Cape Town.

She visited a leftist bookshop and saw my mother and two other Jewish women with casual clothes and frizzy hair passionately arguing about a trade union. Stephanie's own mother would not leave her bedroom without makeup and smart clothes, and this sight in the bookshop radically altered Kemp's view of women and life in general. She later accepted an invitation to have dinner once a week at our guest house.

I imagined, as she spoke, that she was given a deadly dish of chicken soup laced with Marxism. I vaguely remember some of her visits, as well as some visits by Bram Fischer's daughter Ilse. When I was a child, on a visit to Johannesburg my father took me to Fischer's house. I remember him being seated at a table on a wide green lawn. An internationally renowned advocate, he secretly headed the South African Communist Party and was sentenced to life imprisonment after defending Mandela and others. My father regarded him as his mentor, and joined him in prison when he was sentenced to six years and nine months after spending months in solitary confinement.

A student boarder came up to me one day after seeing Stephanie and Ilse visiting the house at different times. He said, "These Communist women are so bloody beautiful," leaving me confounded, as neither Communism nor beautiful women were subjects of open discussion in our family, for reasons I sensed rather than knew.

After her ninetieth birthday my mother told me to write down the name of a World War II pilot she had known. She asked me to make enquiries and find out where he had been killed. I scribbled his name down and mislaid it after failing to get through to the air force museum. She twice asked me what I had found, and I made excuses. I still hope to find a name written on a scrap of paper one day, and have since realised that my tiny frizzy mother apparently had a doomed wartime relationship with an athletic young pilot. Given the casualty rate among pilots there was probably more than one.

When my sister Lynn was researching her book on my parents, I came across extracts of a diary and a group photo from a BBC series on World War II. It concerned someone called Shorty Carneson, who Ntombi agreed might just be Fred; she is exceptionally good at visual comparisons. Our surname is a local corruption of the Portuguese Encarnação, so there are a limited number of Carnesons.

The diary entry was not flattering and referred to a terrified little man with a wound on his chin, running down a trench at El Alamein. He had to take a swig from a flask to carry on. Another entry from the diary referred to him borrowing a pound to go whoring and drinking. Gritting my teeth, I sent the material to Lynn, who published a quote from it in her biography of my parents.

I had assumed Shorty was a nickname for my father, but I later began to doubt the accuracy of the material I sent Lynn, as it clashed with the facts. My father had fought in a series of battles in Italy in which South Africans were noted for their courage, suffering more than four thousand casualties. He learned to speak fluent Italian and worked secretly with the Italian partisans. They helped print political books in isiZulu for black South African soldiers, who were not allowed to bear arms and who got a fraction of the pay given to white soldiers.

When visiting a relative and his wife who lived in Italy, Ntombi and I asked them to take us to Monte Sole, the site of a battle my father had spoken about. He told me about coming across a massacre in which an SS punishment battalion wiped out two villages, after partisans had killed some German officers.

We had lunch with the last living survivor of the families, who had been away on the day of the massacre. For fifty years the man had told the same story. He pointed out the efficiency of the SS. They had lined up the families from one village in the cemetery, as in a photograph: children in front, the women behind, and then the men, so that the machine guns could traverse effectively. The other families had been crowded into a church and blown up. Nobody had ever been punished for the war crime, because, he supposed, all the people had been poor.

In 2019, an internet search helped solve the mystery. Author Douglas Baker had written a book mentioning both my father and his older brother Shorty. The existence of this hidden uncle had never been mentioned to me. My father came to visit his brother at his camp and made friends with Baker, who wrote about the meetings in his gripping memoir, *War, Wine and Valour* (2012). "Fred Carneson, Shorty's brother ... was a remarkable, extrovert young man ... I met up with him in the N.M.R. in 1942 when he would visit our lines, he being then in uniform. He came to visit because his elder brother was a private in the regiment."

According to the book, Shorty was an alcoholic who avoided action at all costs. He was bitter about a violent incident involving my father, who never told me about it. Fred was the first in the railway worker's large family to get a secondary school education, having obtained a scholarship to a prestigious college. The whole family contributed to buying him a uniform and books, which the boys tore to pieces on his first day at school. Later he had to leave school and go to work to support the family.

Shorty attributed Fred's politics to this incident. He had a hatred of the middle classes and intellectuals, and was himself almost illiterate. As the crucial battle of El Alamein progressed, he may have transferred this rage to the German and Italian enemy.

Baker records seeing an exhausted Shorty march towards an enemy machine gun emplacement, dragging a Bren gun behind him. His courage was mentioned in dispatches.

I discovered, as many people do, something about my parents from the way they died. My father died quite quickly from brain cancer. We were living in the Eastern Cape, an eight-hour drive away, so I could only see him once during this time. His sense of humour had not deserted him, and he told me he took comfort from the doctor telling him not to worry, as life was just a sexually transmitted disease. According to my sister's book, on the day of his death, a young man from the Communist Party asked, "Comrade Fred, should I open the curtains for you?" Fred, once a choirboy, responded, "Why not? Perhaps Jesus wants me for a sunbeam."

After the death of my father, Sarah escaped from the retirement village where they had lived and moved to a small flat which she rented in my younger sister Ruth's house by the sea. Her escape had been cheered on by many of the village's conservative British residents. Some appealed to the fiery revolutionary she was, having once too often endured the high-priced slop they were fed when they were moved to the special care facility. Others urged her to stay and lead them against Management. As Ben Elton put it in one of his *Blackadder* scripts, they were ready to wear overalls and break wind in the palaces of the mighty.

It was a wonderful arrangement that she made with my sister Ruth, enriching both of their lives.

When she was ninety-nine, her vital signs began running down, and so Ntombi and I flew to Cape Town from Johannesburg. We found her very weak and a little confused. As she began to slip into the final stage, we feared she might not recognise us.

A nearby hospice had given us a copy of *Crossing the Creek* by Michael Holmes,[3] a useful guide for those who witness the dying process, and everything it described unfolded before our eyes. The family gathered for a meal, where we could take turns to sit with Sarah in her bedroom. She would soon stop eating and drinking. Ntombi mobilised support from the living and from the shades of her ancestors, announcing on Facebook that Sarah would soon be with us no more.

She suddenly revived and insisted on joining us at the table for dinner. We were confused but Sarah was perky, rational and radiant. I have noticed that old ladies get this delicate, beautiful look when they are near death. The meal kept being interrupted by phone calls and messages from friends, relatives and comrades from around the globe. They wanted to know if they were too late and if they should send flowers. The rest of us became more confused and deeply embarrassed, but after taking a couple of the calls Sarah put down the phone. "Oh, they think that I am dead," she said, and roared with laughter, as only Sarah could. We all laughed. She ate a substantial meal before she retired to bed.

She quite soon slipped into that stage where, apart from issuing a few instructions, she communicated almost exclusively with her own parents about traumas in her past, most often silently, and more in Yiddish than in English. She sat up for hours and waved away anyone who stood between her and a window letting light into the passage. She kept saying "Going up", and now and again she made strange gestures and spoke to people we could not see.

When Sarah decided it was time to die, she composed herself, shut down all systems, and died within five minutes. Always in full control, our mother.

Four

We meet in Mazimbu

For the purpose of the present Convention, the term "the crime of apartheid" ... shall apply to the following inhuman acts committed for the purpose of establishing and maintaining domination by one racial group of persons over any other racial group of persons and systematically oppressing them...
– United Nations Convention on Apartheid as a Crime Against Humanity, 1973

I THINK IT WAS Mendi Msimang, an ANC leader, who met me in Mozambique in October 1979 and persuaded me to work at the school which the ANC was building in Tanzania: the Solomon Mahlangu Freedom College (SOMAFCO), named after a young ANC soldier who had been captured and executed.

What impressed me was that he had travelled to Inhambane, where I was then teaching English. It was a seven-hour drive from Mozambique's capital, Maputo, or over an hour by air in a tiny plane. We agreed I would start in January 1980 after visiting my parents and sisters in London. Pay was not discussed, but that did not matter. I was filled with a revolutionary spirit.

SOMAFCO was situated close to the town of Morogoro, on an abandoned sisal estate called Mazimbu, which was loaned to the ANC by the Tanzanian government. It was perhaps five kilometres wide in a beautiful valley formed by mountains that rose behind the town. I worked at the high school there for six years (counting my time spent in London writing a history textbook), developed part of the curriculum, and ran a resource centre that I initiated.

After staying in makeshift accommodation for months, I had been allocated a room in a newly built staff house that I shared with others. I was sitting in the common sitting room when the manager responsible for feeding the students came in with a young woman. She introduced me to Ntombi, explaining that she had studied catering in Zambia and would set up modern kitchens. She was twenty-five and I was thirty-one.

Ntombi's face lit up as she passed a window. The light made her coppery skin glow and her black eyes shine. She was dressed neatly with a hint of efficiency. I was lean and fit, but what Ntombi saw was a balding white man with a thick beard, in bell-bottoms and a crumpled T-shirt.

Something sparked between us: the mix of chemistry, personalities and social processes that feeds the bonding of two humans. Love can grow from it in almost any circumstances, as accidentally as a pearl from a grain of sand. If an oyster could talk, it would tell us stories of irritation, familiarity, and the strengthening of glutinous bonds.

The courtship was brief but active. I was eager and confused, and Ntombi took charge. I had a rival, supported by a mother who was a Leader, whereas my mother was in London. Ntombi was not the kind to be unduly influenced, but seeing my lack of social awareness she made sure that somebody informed me that (a) she was serious, (b) there was a rival, and (c) the person informing me – a senior comrade – would announce she was my supporter.

Ntombi's plans included suggesting a brief ride on the back of my small motorbike along the bumpy track that ran along the mielie fields. A river ran on the other side of the complex, but it was too public. This was unfortunate, as I now know that Ntombi is a deeply traditional Zulu. Courtship involves approaching a girl as she collects firewood near a river. Declaring your love in this well-defined space initiates a series of events that in peacetime leads to the two families, and often clans, being united on many levels.

We married when Ntombi visited me in 1984 in London, where my parents and sisters had gone into exile, one by one, over ten years. I was on sabbatical at the London School of Oriental and African Studies (SOAS), writing a textbook for SOMAFCO. It was a year before the repeal of the Immorality and Mixed Marriages Acts, which outlawed marriage between whites and any other designated race. Our marriage was not recognised as lawful in South Africa, where we would in any case have been jailed as members of the ANC.

Our marriage had other dynamics. As a black person, Ntombi was not considered a citizen of South Africa and was not afforded basic human rights. Members of the ANC were united around a war against apartheid, but it was primarily a nationalist movement that had grown out of the misery and oppression of the African majority, who were united by similar languages, traditions, clan systems, and kingdoms. I did not speak isiZulu or any other African language.

I was uncertain what to do when I heard Ntombi's father wanted lobola in the form of cattle, which in the eyes of many is the only way to bind the two families and secure full rights over the couple's children. From his side, he sent us a diamond ring from Swaziland, where he was based. I came across the ANC treasurer general in London and asked him what to do. He brushed past me, saying, "Tell him he is mad. We are in the middle of a war." Years later I was finally able to pay lobola.

Within two years, in 1986, we had our first child, Busisiwe, or Busi as she is known. She was born in the government hospital in Morogoro. The beds were dirty, with hardly any linen, and most were already occupied. Ntombi birthed our daughter on the floor, which looked cleaner. I was not allowed in until after the birth. The nurses were tough and expert. Ntombi now denies telling me that one nurse shouted at a screaming woman, "Yes, you like it when things go in like a banana but not when they come out like a pineapple."

One risk for a country hosting refugees is that the exiles may be pursued by those from whom they are running away. This was true under apartheid: ANC exiles living in countries bordering South Africa were attacked, and hundreds of citizens of those countries died in the cross-border raids. Millions died in Angola and Mozambique because of civil wars sponsored by the South African state and its Cold War allies.

We usually felt safe in Mazimbu, apart from rumours of sabotage and spies and the secret activities of ANC intelligence. It was not near the sea and I assumed we were out of range of the South African Air Force.

Then, shortly after the birth of Busi, we were told that bombers could refuel in a third country and reach us. It was believed that they would attack us at dawn. For some weeks, Ntombi and Busi, with other new mothers and their babies as well as pregnant women, were bused away from Mazimbu before sunrise and returned later in the day.

We were advised to take precautions, without being given much advice and no training. I dug a deep pit outside our house with a sloping trench leading to it. If there was a raid, my idea was to clutch the infant Busi to my chest and roll down the ramp. The attack never happened, but the memory awakens the senses that exiles evolve. Your ears are tuned to pick up gossip and the occasional fact. Your nose sniffs the political air to pick up the scent of trouble from within the exile community, from international developments, and in the host country.

SOMAFCO soon became part of a larger project supported by the global anti-apartheid movement. Eventually we added a primary school and had the largest furniture factory and piggery in Tanzania, as well as a clothing factory. Many of the children in the nursery school were born in the government hospital in town.

In Mazimbu there was a flourishing of poetry, music, drama and dance. The martial arts were taught by an exiled karate champion who had joined us from the United States. Many of the students toured the world with the ANC's professional Amandla music, drama and dance group, and South African artists began to visit the growing complex, and among them Abdullah Ibrahim, formerly Dollar Brand.

More remarkable, but less noticed, was the cultural undergrowth that emerged in a hothouse of twenty or so square kilometres. Ntombi had studied catering in Lusaka and had been sent from Zambia to establish modern kitchens. I asked Ashia, one of the Tanzanian workers she employed, how things were going. She replied, "Mimi sebenza too much," packing Kiswahili, isiZulu and English into four words meaning "I am working too much".

The linguistic stew grew richer daily as the children of exiles arrived, some speaking Portuguese and Shangaan. There were also anti-apartheid volunteers who spoke Dutch, Finnish, Swedish and German. Older ANC students returned, some talking to one another in Russian, Spanish or Bulgarian.

English was the common language, but a dialect quickly began to emerge. For instance, our clothing needs were met by clawing through huge piles of clothing called *mpando*, donated by anti-apartheid groups. *Ukumpanda* is the isiZulu verb meaning "to scratch like a chicken". I was told that the students had given me a nickname meaning "he who walks in two directions at once", based on my fondness for selecting bell-bottom trousers. I only ironed my underclothing, and that was because of eggs that mango flies, also known as skin maggot flies, liked to lay in clothes while they were drying.

Fornication was described by words associated with food, such as chowing or eating cake, perhaps because eating was another of our few pleasures. The term "comrade" was and is defined very loosely. We both laughed when we were told that God had punished a comrade for chowing the wife of a colleague and for neglecting to iron his underwear. Worms had hatched from the eggs the flies laid in his clothes and they burrowed into his genitals.

Ntombi was disgusted by my teaching in sloppy clothes, and she was annoyed when looking in vain for a seam when ironing my bell-bottoms. She referred to this problem when subtly attacking my two worst character defects – my lack of backbone and a tendency to wander about in a dreamy and unfocused state. Since she has grown old and irritable, Ntombi mounts very direct attacks.

We were privileged to have working among us the Ngwenya, meaning "crocodile". They were so called because in the 1960s they were the first ANC soldiers to be trained, and they crossed the Limpopo River which runs between South Africa and what is now Zimbabwe. These soldiers had among them expert drivers, builders and medical officers. Some had spent almost twenty years in exile, with no end in sight until the unbanning of the ANC in 1990. Mostly men, they were friendly and resourceful, and had survived great hardships.

Some are in their eighties now and becoming scarce, thinned out before and after returning from exile by war, disease, poverty, sudden wealth and bad luck. Some died in Mazimbu, among them a man the students called Uncle Eli, a name probably based on his nom de guerre. He told me a story that illustrates the uncertainties of exile. He was sent from the Soviet Union to China to do specialist training when a frontier war broke out between the two countries. The Chinese politely dumped him over a border somewhere, and Eli was not sure which country he was in. He had a couple of dollars, a dark skin and a dodgy travel document, and spoke perhaps six languages but none that were immediately useful. He knew that he might have to go around war zones or militarised frontiers. It took him several months, but he made his way back to Africa and the ANC, which had established offices in many African countries.

Eli was unlucky enough to be killed by the only large wild animal ever seen by us in Mazimbu. Successive groups of villagers had driven a young hippo along a river that ran by our settlement. It had escaped from a game reserve many kilometres away. Eli was returning from a shebeen with his comrades at sunset and saw the frantic animal looking up at him as he walked along the riverbank. Eli was a lover of animals and he kept a collection of them, including live snakes. Fascinated, he climbed a tree to get a closer look and the branch on to which he was holding broke.

To varying degrees, the Ngwenya had integrated into Tanzanian society, marrying into local families or entering into various informal arrangements. Other exiles had brought wives or husbands from as far as the United States or the outer Soviet republics. Some of these marriages were inspirational and survived the cross-currents and rip tides of class, race and culture, but many were shipwrecked.

On reflection, the determining factor seemed to be the extent to which values and aspirations were shared by a couple. I realise that other people may see Ntombi and me in this light, even though we are both South Africans. Little do they know how many hippos are down there looking up at us, and how fragile are the branches we hang on to.

One of the fears of exiles and soldiers is that they will die where nobody they love will ever know how they died or be able to find their graves. In 1981, a year or so before Ntombi arrived back in Mazimbu and met me, I found myself two hundred kilometres away in Dar es Salaam on 16 December, which was designated as Heroes Day by the ANC.

I joined other ANC exiles. We stood in a sweltering, overgrown cemetery, listening to the understated humour and voice of Boston, a senior Ngwenya who worked at the ANC office in Dar. He was the only one who knew exactly where all exiled South Africans were buried; he himself is now long dead.

"By that tree, we buried a man who had a small infection of the foot, which he neglected, and septicaemia took him. One day we will proudly present the bones of all our heroes to their families back home." Boston paused and looked thoughtful. "We must remember one comrade from the Pan Africanist Congress, who is buried in that corner. He was a good man, and you can say he is trying to join us underground."

The apartheid state had declared 16 December to be the Day of the Covenant, a public holiday that I knew as Dingaan's Day when I was a schoolboy. I was taught at school that on this day, at the Battle of Blood River, the Zulu king Dingaan and his people were punished by God for treacherously killing a column of Voortrekkers led by Piet Retief. Ntombi heard a different story from her clan elders, who told her that superior tactics were used to defeat the heavily armed invaders who had a huge appetite for land and forced labour.

Exiles feel safer in a community of their own, such as Mazimbu, especially if they are surrounded by their culture. There is a long list of South African poets, writers, artists and musicians who were driven into exile. Living in isolation and cut off from their roots, many died from misery and self-destruction.

As a student in London, I saved up to spend evenings at 100 Oxford Street, a club where such folk gathered. Twice I witnessed a famed South African musician descend into a crazed drunken state and topple from the stage. The second time, I was sitting near a well-known artist who shook his head, and continued sketching.

Ntombi had far more experience of being in exile in Africa, having stayed in Mazimbu when the project started and there was just one teacher. She had already lived in Swaziland and Mozambique, and was later sent to Sierra Leone, Cuba and Zambia. In each place she plugged into a growing network of ANC exiles, some of whom she knew already, and others of whom were related to her family. She was introduced to local contacts and communities.

Ntombi understood much of the culture of the Tanzanian communities around Mazimbu and Morogoro, where ANC exiles had lived since the 1960s. She explained that cowrie shells hanging on the door of a hut were there to ensure fertility. Green branches carried by a procession meant someone was graduating to adulthood. She had grown up in a similar rural area and she learned the basics of Kiswahili rapidly. Almost all southern African languages share a similar structure and some vocabulary, although Kiswahili has many elements of Arabic.

I had spent most of my exile in England and, like most white South Africans, I have poor African language skills, mainly because of our attitude and being locked into white communities. White kids were not taught African languages at school. I could converse in Portuguese quite fluently, having worked in Portugal and Mozambique, but that was of little use in Tanzania.

My contact with the ANC outside London was minimal. In Mozambique I had worked in Inhambane, far from the capital where most exiles were based. I occasionally visited families I got to know in local communities but spent most of my time teaching or interacting with other *cooperantes*, who had volunteered to work in the newly independent state.

By the time we left in early 1987 to study and work in England, Mazimbu was full of every kind of exile. Anti-apartheid volunteers worked with us as teachers and builders from the UK, the US, both Germanies, Holland and the Nordic countries. It was evolving into a kaleidoscopic reflection of what we imagined a future South Africa would be like. Nobody was sure whether they would live to celebrate the fall of apartheid. It was a special place, and strong relationships were forged among the people who lived there, which are still active forty years later.

Five

A visit to Ntombi's roots

In the blessings coming from the foundation,
Cloud-like branches
Small soil
Small House
Hoping to live
To live in centuries
This century-old family
– Bulent Karaalioglu, "Poor and Poor Villager"

TEN YEARS AFTER WE MET, we returned to South Africa in 1993, with many other exiles. Ntombi's mother Nomvula left the white family she was working for in Ladysmith and came to live with us in Cape Town before the birth of our son Sipho. She had not seen Ntombi since she went into exile in the 1970. She provided Ntombi with a mother, our children with a grandmother, and our family with practical assistance and a moral and emotional centre.

As we both approached retirement in 2018, Ntombi reminded me that after we returned to South Africa, she and Gogo had followed me as I hopped from job to job, moving from one white suburb to another. We visited my family regularly, but we had only been in touch with her family now and again. "Now it is my time," she said.

A few weeks later, Ntombi told me, "I must go and attend to the grave of my twin sister Thembalihle and do a ceremony." I had no idea what she was talking about, never having heard that Ntombi had a sister, alive or dead. The only sibling I knew was Khumbulani, her younger brother. We were to take Gogo with us. Not only was she the mother of the dead child, but she had hardly seen her surviving relatives since moving in with us.

The grave she had to visit and clean was in Kwamteyi, where Ntombi had spent most of her childhood, a small settlement spread over tribal trust land in the district of Ladysmith. The name was not on any map I could find, which tells its own story. She started packing without giving me any details. I did not probe, as Ntombi undoubtedly had reasons why she had not revealed her dead sister to me for thirty years.

We arrived after a six-hour drive and first greeted her uncle Abel Mdluli, an active eighty-nine-year-old who practises as a traditional healer, or *inyanga*. As he is the oldest of her father's brothers, she refers to him as Mkhulu, a short form of Baba Mkhulu, or Great Father. She is close to him, and I respect and like him.

In Zulu culture, all paternal uncles and aunts are your fathers and mothers, and their children are your brothers and sisters. The concept of cousin better fits your relationship with maternal relatives, but even then it is not the same.

From Abel's cluster of crumbling mud and cement buildings, we drove across the local tarred road, which was mostly free of potholes, went up a short dirt road and parked in front of a steep, rocky hill that Ntombi remembered as a mountain.

Holding a hoe and a bag of plants and toys in one hand, Ntombi used a stick to clamber among the boulders while I stayed by the car. The hillside had not been disturbed for a long time and I feared snakes, but mostly I sensed she needed to be alone. Bending at the waist, exactly like the peasants in Van Gogh's potato fields, she began to move rocks and clear away small bushes.

I heard her performing a ritual after planting her cuttings around the grave and emptying a bottle of water over them. In the centre she placed the toys and the bottle and angled a solar-powered lantern.

It was late afternoon when she finished, and the sun was setting behind the hill. As she came back to the car, the lantern switched on and a faint beam shone upwards. We headed back to our home, mostly in silence.

Over the next eighteen months Ntombi told me stories about her family history. Gogo listened with intense interest and Ntombi explained details in isiZulu now and again. Occasionally Gogo would add to the story. Gogo's English is better than my isiZulu, but I sometimes think I catch the gist of their conversation when they mention some words I recognise.

After our two children left home, we lost the habit of sitting down to eat dinner together. Ntombi would retreat to the bedroom with a plate of food to nurse her. She worked social media using her phone, while watching TV and listening to the radio. I would take my plate to my desk or the TV room, and Gogo would eat alone or go to her bedroom. During the Covid-19 lockdown, Ntombi began telling more stories about her childhood. It became an important part of our day and pulled us together again.

Not usually a shy person, Ntombi would slyly and shyly mention something about her childhood near the end of a meal, and then enthusiastically expand on the point, often acting out the stories with a change of voice and fluid gestures. She could become King Shaka, a river or a donkey's left ear in the space of a minute. I was astonished that I had always taken this skill for granted. It was magical.

From the stories, I began to piece together the history of Ntombi's birth and the untimely death of two of her siblings. The second death was that of Sifiso, a boy who died in childbirth after

Ntombi was born. I realised how little I knew and understood about Ntombi, and how it was that she survived her childhood, exile from South Africa, and then life with me.

Ntombi was born in September 1957 into a family and community that retained many of the values and features of traditional Zulu society, while its development continued to be affected by the colonial machinery of the apartheid state. Until she was twelve, she lived mainly with her father's family in Kwamteyi. She then left to join her father Shoti Lukhele in Swaziland. He had separated from her mother after he went into exile in Swaziland.

The scattered homesteads are thirty-six kilometres from Ladysmith, the nearest large town. There is not much evidence of a vision or a plan at the Kwamteyi end of the broad valley. Because of apartheid forced removals, too many people began competing for dusty land and shrinking water resources. They now rely on pensions and other grants, and on support from family members such as Ntombi, who have settled in urban areas and joined the new black middle class.

Historically, such areas were deliberately undeveloped to force people into migrant labour. However, when visiting rural South Africa, I could see that other rural communities were visibly better off because families, clans, leaders and administration were stronger. I began to understand Ntombi's passion for building her family, clan and the community she was born into.

When she was a child, Ntombi's survival and development depended to a significant extent on the support she had from her four grandparents. She often visited her paternal grandmother Nobango, known as Beauty, who lived in Steadville, a crowded location just outside Ladysmith. The Indian family who owned a trading store and a bus company near Kwamteyi was friendly with her father Shoti, and Ntombi was given lifts, sitting near the driver.

She also visited her mother's family, who lived near Ladysmith in a fertile valley called Ekuphumuleni, meaning "place of rest". During her first period of exile in Tanzania, Ntombi was listening to the

ANC's Radio Freedom when she heard that all the black families in the valley were being forced to abandon their land, which was given to white farmers without a cent of compensation.

The police and army arrived, bulldozed their houses, and forced them onto lorries. They were dumped on arid wasteland in a rural settlement twenty kilometres from Ladysmith. Not only had they lost their farms and houses, but suddenly they were forced to take an expensive bus ride to reach shops or a clinic or go to work. In a few hours, Ntombi's maternal roots had been cut and her mother's family scattered and impoverished economically, socially and spiritually.

In Kwamteyi, Ntombi's grandfather Maxen Lukhele carried out the decisions of the chief's court when he was not working as a cook at a mine in Kimberley. Both of Ntombi's grandfathers had the biggest houses in their respective family homesteads, in the form of a large dwelling, surrounded by clusters of smaller huts that accommodated their sons and their wives, who lived with their children. The family fields were close to nearby rivers and there was common grazing and woodlands.

One day Maxen was sitting outside his house and called the infant Ntombi to come to him. She was wearing a denim skirt held up by shoulder straps and, as she advanced, planted each foot firmly before her as if she was going zi-zi-zi. He gave her a Lukhele clan name, Zika.

On the other side of Ladysmith was Ekuphumuleni, the valley where her maternal grandparents lived. One day, when she was visiting them, her grandfather Samuel Mbele was sitting outside his house and he called Ntombi. The infant moved towards him in a determined way, and he gave her an Mbele clan name, Nkhelekele, meaning "an unstoppable flood".

I told Ntombi that I would have loved to have met these two wise men and discussed the qualities of their granddaughter with them.

Each homestead was on the side of a hill in front of a thornbush kraal for livestock, which had spiritual and social significance.

When visitors approached any homestead, they had to announce who they were before being allowed to proceed. They had to mention their clans and who their grandparent and parents were. The family would follow her grandfather Maxen past the kraal in a line, and repeat the names after he shouted them: Lukhele! Mdluli! and so on. In this way he informed the ancestors about the visitors so they could welcome them and ensure that the visit went well.

Nomvula lost two children by the time she was in her early twenties. The first to die was a girl named Thembalihle, which means "a beautiful hope". She was born in December and died after spending just two months on earth. After the birth of Ntombi she lost Sifiso, a boy who died in childbirth while she was staying with her family. Her last-born was Khumbulani, who survived to become Ntombi's younger brother. A retired police captain, he gets on well with his sister. He lives in another province, and we see him or his family members quite often.

Ntombi calculates that her own conception must have occurred when Shoti was allowed home from his work in Johannesburg for his Christmas break. She believes that when Nomvula became pregnant with her, so soon after giving birth to her sister, her breast milk dried up and there was not enough food to keep her infant sister alive.

The young mother received little money from her husband. In part this was because he prioritised other needs, but mostly it was because wages under apartheid were below what was needed to support a migrant worker's family. This was based on the official lie that rural Africans had the means to grow enough food to feed their families.

To give her second baby a better chance of survival, the pregnant Nomvula went to give birth to Ntombi at the house of Beauty, her mother-in-law. The three-roomed, red-brick house was in Steadville location, outside Ladysmith. One advantage was that it was near a clinic where Nomvula would have access to nurses. At that time, Kwamteyi was far from any clinic or hospital.

Last time we visited Ntombi's family, we drove through Steadville to drop a friend off. She told us to wait, and came back with a large green gourd and a fat pumpkin, grown in her sandy yard. Ntombi told me that when she was a child, there was a yellow cling peach tree and a plum tree in Beauty's yard. Every year Beauty produced stacks of bottled peaches.

Her real business was in the house, where she illegally brewed traditional beer, usually finding time to hide it in the nearby river when there was a police raid. She and the other women would clean paraffin tins to store beer in and bury them, covering them with turf. The police would use sticks to thump on the ground to try to discover where the liquor was hidden.

The government wanted to derive maximum revenue from their official beer halls, where police spies were abundant. They feared the independence the income from shebeens gave Africans and the conversation that went unrecorded every evening when patrons drank beer and talked politics. They wanted shebeen owners like Beauty to work in factories or as servants in the houses of whites, just as Gogo was forced to do after her husband left her.

Those patrons who were migrant workers in Ladysmith got to sleep on mats that covered the living-room floor. "When I stayed there, you had to step carefully around them," Ntombi recalled. Every day, from out of the tiny kitchenette came huge pots of maize pap with gravy and cabbage. The leftovers from dinner were consumed for breakfast. The workers woke up at dawn to go to the municipal wash house to shower and get ready for work.

The income Beauty derived from the shebeen sustained the family, kept Ntombi alive in Nomvula's womb, and helped feed and clothe her through the first years of her life. Ntombi is always angry when she hears experts praise the nutritional value of African traditional beer. She remembers the violent police raids and the beer being poured down the drain or dumped in the river, after her grandmother had spent days brewing it.

"What I hate is how blacks are still called barbaric for brewing beer and treating themselves with herbs. The herbs are sold now as expensive cosmetics and medicines. And they have found that the beer is full of important vitamins."

Nomvula's family, the Mbeles, had assisted her with money. When the infant Ntombi fell ill, Shoti came to visit from Johannesburg and Nomvula handed him the money so he could get a bus to Ladysmith and buy medicine. Shoti was well dressed and Gogo warned him not to use the money to go with nurses.

When Nomvula followed him to the clinic, she caught him walking and talking with a nurse. She grabbed him by the tie and hit him, telling him that her brothers would finish him if he dared to beat her. The medicine was bought and may have saved the infant Ntombi's life.

The illness got worse after Gogo returned with Ntombi to Kwamteyi, and the family consulted an *inyanga*. He advised them to tell the spirits not to take her, and explain that she had a "twin" sister who had already died. To persuade the spirits, a burial was arranged using Thembalihle's clothes, drenched in the water used to wash Ntombi. When I learned about this ceremony, I understood why Ntombi always refers to Thembalihle as her twin.

Recently there was a political scandal because F.W. de Klerk, the last apartheid state president, denied that the apartheid state had committed genocide. Under pressure, he eventually retracted his statement. I assume that he was reminded of the statistics: about one in four black children in rural areas used to die from malnutrition and preventable diseases. This genocide was a planned consequence of dozens of apartheid policies: the pass laws, the migrant labour system, forced removals, and deliberate lack of development.

Among the victims who died were Nomvula's children, Thembalihle and Sifiso, whom Nomvula had carried in her womb for nine months while doing her heavy load of work. Ntombi often thinks about her dead siblings and wishes they were alive so that they could strengthen and lead the family.

Six
Abandonment

Abandonment issues arise when an individual has a strong fear of losing loved ones. A fear of abandonment is a form of anxiety. It often begins in childhood when a child experiences a traumatic loss.
– Jayne Leonard, Medical News Today, 2020

ONE OF MY EARLIEST memories of abandonment was missing my father for long periods, which must have been between 1956, when I was five, and 1959. He was one of the one hundred and fifty-six accused at the Treason Trial, held in Johannesburg, twelve hundred kilometres away from Cape Town where we lived. I was not aware of my father being among the leaders who were rounded up, or how the trial was conducted, or that he could have been hanged because the charge was treason. Then in 1960, when I was nine, both of my parents abandoned me for a year – or at least it seemed that way to me.

I recall the pain and sobbing into the bosom of a family friend called Sadie at our guest house in Cape Town. She cursed the government, which had used a State of Emergency to force my father into hiding and jail my mother. I visited her twice in two different prisons and was taken to meet my father at a secret rendezvous on the side of Table Mountain near the university. He looked healthy and relaxed and wore glasses and a moustache to disguise himself. The security forces never found him although he stayed around the corner from the largest police station in Cape Town.

The full might of the apartheid state had not yet been unleashed against its white opponents, and there were still families of sympathisers willing to care for their children. In our case, my younger sister Ruth and I were given refuge by a warm and welcoming Jewish family. I can remember a bear-like man called Nathie Horwitz, and his wife Chrystal, who was tallish and slender with a smooth skin. I was fascinated by Nathie, who hesitantly but sincerely performed rituals on Yom Kippur and Rosh Hashanah. At these ceremonies I remember there were candlesticks, wine, matzos and sweets, and prayers chanted in a growling language.

My sister told me that Chrystal did art with us, but I remember nothing. Years later I heard that they had divorced. I felt rather than saw that she was nervous, but that may well have been the State of Emergency. Other memories are hidden by whatever means my subconscious uses to protect me. It usually knows best, and there is always a price to pay if you force it to open its store of memories.

Abandonment was built into the fabric and structure of Ntombi's life by the apartheid state. It told her in many ways that she must abandon the idea that she had the same rights as a citizen like myself, who was classified as a white European. She was classified by various South African laws as a Native, a Non-European and a Bantu. The last term simply means "people" in Nguni languages such as isiZulu, but was used in a highly derogatory way.

As a child Ntombi was confused and wondered how being called a person could be an insult. I imagine her in a post office, queuing at a sign marked Non-Europeans, and a white child asking his mother loudly why a Bantu was in the room. In rural areas black people were served through a shop window or had to leave the room if a white person came in.

Ntombi was allocated to the Zulu ethnic group and put under a government-appointed chief whose name appeared in a pass book along with stamps obliging her to live in the "homeland" reserved for Zulus. Black South Africans called the hated book a *dompas*, meaning "stupid pass" in Afrikaans. The system was labyrinthine and arbitrary, staffed mostly by corrupt and poorly educated Afrikaners.

The mountain of injustice resting on the child Ntombi was put in place by Dutch and British colonial regimes over three hundred years and perfected by Afrikaners and English-speaking whites under apartheid. Every year, all over southern Africa, millions of black men abandoned their families in rural settlements and went to work in the mines, farms and factories of South Africa. Ntombi's father worked in a factory in Johannesburg, a day's journey away. Most years she saw him and her working relatives only at Easter and at Christmas.

The four million South Africans who were classified as white had rights to eighty-seven per cent of the land. As the population grew, forced removals were undertaken to concentrate forty million Africans on the fragments of land demarcated for the different black nations and clans.

When Ntombi was about five, this policy led to an influx of people into Kwamteyi, and to the family having to abandon their houses and rebuild further from the river on which they depended for water. The pattern of life she loves to recall was broken. Her father would send little money, and with less food being produced they often went hungry. The levels of violence and insecurity rose, clan fighting clan, and families sometimes had to go into hiding, especially when men returned from the mines during Easter and Christmas.

There was a period when Ntombi stayed with an aunt who produced more food but lived far from services. She walked hours every day to and from primary school, crossing rivers where floods and crocodiles sometimes took children. "I had to undress, put everything on my head and dress again on the other side. There were good men who could swim, and they helped us with ropes and floating logs, but when there was a flood, a child could disappear. They became one of the uncounted."

Gathering wood or collecting water was arduous, with Ntombi balancing heavy loads on her head, carefully treading the stony paths. After the aunt and her family harvested their crops, they would load donkeys with the bags of maize they had grown and lead the donkeys to the mill to have it ground. The remainder of the bags would be loaded onto the people's heads.

"Children today have no idea what we had to do. We had to walk over hills and around big rocks, guiding the donkeys and balancing the bags. It was at least four hours each way. You kept one eye on a corner of the bag, so when there was a hole or a rock you adjusted the load with small movements. We would sing a song about the crying and behaviour of donkeys. They would stop to urinate, or go the wrong way around a big rock."

The family of Ntombi's mother Nomvula lived much closer to Ladysmith, in a green valley. When she visited her mother's family, Ntombi felt she was back in the time before their forced removal, with a rhythm of life that made her feel that she belonged and was secure.

Ntombi remembers her father being one of the Khongolosi, the name given to men who were members of the African National Congress. They regularly climbed the large rocky hill that rose behind their homestead, carrying food and water. Every child knew they were meeting in secret because of the police and their spies. They heard singing and slogans being shouted, and sometimes they helped carry food and water up the hill.

In 1960, Ntombi's father abandoned her mother and, because of his underground work, went into exile in Swaziland. She later divorced him. Nomvula was forced to work for white families in Ladysmith, and Ntombi stayed with various family members, often missing months of school.

The Lukhele family decided Ntombi would have a better future if she went to join her father and stepmother and attend boarding school in Swaziland. Her brother Khumbulani was already there.

She was twelve when her father's oldest brother arranged for her to be taken to the house of a family member in Soweto. She had to stay with them for some months, until someone could be found to take her to Swaziland. The family had so little money they had to make do with a small packet of maize every other day. The children were given a few cents to buy a slice of bread with polony and atchar on their way to school. Ntombi lost more months of schooling, and had to remain in the house, looking for crumbs of burnt pap at the bottom of a pot. Thus began her time of abandonment, loneliness and great hardships.

In 1965, with my father's arrest, solitary confinement and approaching trial, and with the ongoing harassment of my mother, my parents decided that I should leave South Africa to attend a boarding school in England. My older sister Lynn was studying and working in London and had arranged with one of the Cadbury family to sponsor me to attend Leighton Park, a Quaker private school in the town of Reading. Amnesty International arranged for me to live with an English family in London during holidays.

With my sixteenth birthday approaching, I abandoned my home, friends and country, leaving my father in prison and my younger sister and mother to face a murderous state. I had narrowly missed being killed when someone fired a shot into our living room, through the wooden shutters. It was one of the many tactics used to intimidate enemies of the state. Friends and comrades were in exile or prison. Sympathisers who used to assist us were paralysed by fear.

Little of this was explained to me, and I experienced it as a feeling of stress and dread, which has never quite left me. I frequently had a nightmare: a huge rhinoceros would smash through my bedroom door. When I was under great pressure, not long before retirement, that dream came back. I felt trapped for a while in a place where there is fear and panic attacks and no hope. Then survival mechanisms kicked in. I began to analyse my situation objectively and take whatever steps were necessary to deal with the problem.

The last thing I saw of South Africa, standing at the rail of a Union-Castle liner in 1966, was Robben Island. My parents, because of their underground work, kept me away from details of the struggle, and I did not know about the political prisoners on the island. But I do remember a terrible feeling of loss that rose like a stone in my throat.

Years later I was working in Mozambique and friends drove me to Swaziland in their Land Rover to buy a motorbike. On the way someone showed me a fence and told me South Africa was on the other side. The same feeling came back as I looked through the mesh at an identical expanse of bushveld.

There were periods when, for several of our teenage years, Ntombi and I found refuge in our respective boarding schools. There was little news or contact with my family in South Africa, but I had my sister Lynn in London, who visited me perhaps once a month. I would spend hours on Sundays looking out for Lynn's old Ford, both ashamed and proud of it when I saw it parked among the Jags and Bentleys. She had got the class she was teaching to decorate her pale-grey car with wet leaves and spray over them with darker paint.

A feeling of isolation and loneliness at times overwhelmed me, despite the friends I made and the supportive family I stayed with in London during holidays. White as I was, and English speaking, there was a cultural divide I never quite managed to cross. The family were active in the Labour Party, and the first day I stayed there I was introduced to an elderly friend of theirs who worked in Parliament.

"What do you do?" I asked him.

He drew himself up and looked proud. "I carry the mace when they open Parliament. They call me Black Rod."

"Oh, you mean you are a lackey," I responded, remembering a word from a fairy tale.

I was surprised by the look of discomfort on the faces in the room as he tried to explain his duties to me.

At the school I struggled to do maths and science Ordinary Levels, which were pitched higher than their equivalent in South Africa. I did much better in English and asked if I could go on to do English, history and biology for my Advanced Levels, which were on par with the content studied by first-year undergraduates in South Africa. The principal, a thin man whom the boys called "The Skull", refused this request. He reluctantly explained that a colonial boy could not be expected to understand English and history. He mentioned he had obtained a double first at Oxford. His face was like parchment stretched over bone, and I remembered him when I saw the wizard Voldemort in a Harry Potter movie.

Ntombi experienced the same feelings of loneliness and isolation, despite being warmly received into the Catholic mission community and having many relatives in Swaziland (now called eSwatini). Ntombi's father (known as Mpiko in Swaziland) had married into the Swazi royal family, and his wife Princess Msalela took Ntombi by bus to the mission school.

Ntombi had stayed in Johannesburg for eighteen months, waiting for someone to take her to Swaziland. She lost so much schooling that she had to repeat the whole of primary school in Swaziland, where she was taught in English for the first time.

Her love of education is deep, and she persisted. Ntombi was nearly twenty years old by the time she completed three years of high school and passed her Junior Certificate exam. Gogo collected enough money to send her a parcel containing a suit of clothes. I recently saw a small photo showing her at the time of her twenty-first birthday. An enlarged copy on the finest art canvas now looks down on us from our lounge wall.

Ntombi was largely estranged from her father, who never visited the school or supported her. She often felt like a poor and unwelcome relative when she visited his home during the holidays. The princess was strict but fair in assigning Ntombi's duties and expected her own child to work with Ntombi and carry out the same heavy schedule of chores.

One evening, Ntombi, Gogo and I were having supper, and I hoped to harvest more stories about her life at boarding school. She always traced her ability to live frugally by having had to survive on what my Yiddishe mother called the smell of an oil rag. I went to wash some dishes and Ntombi observed me through the kitchen door. "You are that thing your mother used to call some people: extravagant. You wash the dishes with so much soap they cannot see your hands. You have too many bad habits."

I began to worry about which of my habits she would pick on next. It began with a giggle which I tried to disguise as a cough. "John is laughing," said Gogo, pleased that I was happy. I spluttered out bits of pizza and managed to say, "How many bad habits am I allowed to have?"

Ntombi smiled and pulled me down memory lane towards a time when characters like her were carved out of solid sweat. "You met MaMdaweni before she died, when we went to that funeral in Soweto. My father's brothers and sisters were like my fathers and mothers.

"She lived near my father in Swaziland. I had stinking armpits. You would think my father would give me deodorants, but I got nothing. Instead MaMdaweni saved me. She showed me how to smear that blue soap on my armpits. When I talk about soap, I remember that blue type with black spots we had when I was child. You hardly find it now, but it got clothes very white." Ntombi paused, then carried on, "No stink, the whole day."

Ntombi's stories often revolved around how she survived at school, drying each part of herself with a small piece of cloth, then wringing it dry before moving to the next area of skin. Or adding one sardine a day to her mound of maize pap from a tin she had brought back from a rare visit across the border to her mother. She made cookies and cooked dinners for the priests, who let her keep some of the food.

Nomvula would save up from her domestic worker's wages until she could send money for Ntombi to visit her in Ladysmith or else she sent her food and clothes. She gave her daughter supplies to take back with her, and clothes to share with her younger brother and local relatives. A tube of toothpaste would have to last Ntombi half a year. "Use the brush more," Ntombi tells me when she sees me brushing my teeth. "It is like you think the toothpaste must do your work."

At age sixteen she was about to transfer to a secondary school, and loneliness and neglect had bitten her once too often. She confronted her father, saying she wanted nothing to do with him, and that she belonged henceforth to her mother's family and clan. This was an almost unthinkable step for a child to take. Marriage is a complicated contract between families and clans, sealed by ceremonies involving the ancestors. Lobola is paid in cattle to the wife's family as compensation for losing her as a worker and for strengthening the relationship between the families. One beast, for example, is slaughtered to feed the groom's family.

Ntombi went to stay with MaMdaweni's older sister, who had moved from South Africa to a border town in Swaziland. She was warmly welcomed, although there were some days when a few leaves of spinach were all they had to share and eat with their pap.

"If you saw her, you would say she was a real beauty, very black skin, with a fine body and face structure. Her husband brought her and the children from South Africa. Left them with nothing. He was another man, like my father, who went away to work and never sent money. But she was proud. You know those maize sacks, we would use them to smear white clay on the walls.

"These kids today know nothing of work. When I was at the Catholic mission school, we would scrub the church from here to where our front gate is, on our knees. Those were real priests, visiting the people in the villages, not like now with greedy stomachs and ten per cents of your money. Why are people so greedy today? Finish your pizza."

The independence of Mozambique in 1975 and the uprising of youth in South Africa in 1976 led to the intensification of the anti-apartheid struggle on all fronts, led by the ANC. Ntombi's father

Mpiko (known as Shoti in South Africa) played an important and courageous role, helping to spirit activists out of the country and bring fighters and weapons in. As he had married into the Swazi royal family, his relationship with King Sobhuza was important.

Mpiko acquired a homestead, two shops and a farm, which he made available to the ANC. From 1975, Ntombi started looking after the people in safe houses and at great risk couriered money, mainly between Zambia and Swaziland. The relationship with her father was partly repaired.

Her grandfather Maxen Lukhele came to Swaziland to look after his son's cattle and arranged a ceremony so that the ancestors would connect with Ntombi. He asked them always to guide and protect her, and he predicted that she would travel the world, north, south, east and west, before returning home to South Africa. And so it came to pass.

The war against apartheid was essentially anti-colonial, with the ANC exploiting the close ties between communities on both sides of South Africa's borders. To stop the flows of people and weapons, the regime stepped up operations in neighbouring states, ranging from assassination, kidnapping and bombings to military raids.

In 1977, shortly after Ntombi obtained her Junior Certificate, she was given twenty-four hours to throw a few things into a plastic bag and abandon Swaziland. She was driven with other cadres to the comparative safety of Maputo, the capital of Mozambique.

From there, students such as Ntombi were moved around the world, as her grandfather had foretold. They studied when they could find a friendly country, and they assisted the ANC. Others, like Ntombi's brother, became soldiers in the armed wing of the ANC, Umkhonto we Sizwe, or the Spear of the Nation.

From Mozambique, Ntombi was moved to Tanzania, Zambia, Sierra Leone and Cuba; and back to Zambia and then to Tanzania, where I met her in 1983. The ANC established SOMAFCO there because of the scattering of young exiles around the world. They needed to be prepared for the new South Africa, when that day came. Ntombi never formally completed senior high school but managed to get into a further education college in Zambia to study catering.

As for me, I still think Black Rod is a lackey, and that colonial boys can do well at English and history. I proved that by leaving the private school for a despised technical college in London, where I found the teaching to be excellent. I obtained three Bs for my A-levels: English, history and sociology. It was enough in those days to get me an offer from any university I applied to. I ended up at the London School of Economics, and after completing a BSc Honours in sociology, I did a one-year postgraduate teaching diploma at the Institute of Education in London.

Seven

I married my grandmother

If we can give to urban people the peasant's love of nature and their deep understanding on the matter of nature's importance, the salvation of our Earth will be easier!
– Mehmet Murat Ildan, Turkish playwright and novelist (b. 1965)[4]

I DO NOT FIND IT surprising that men often marry women who are like their mothers. Most men start life with their mother being their larder, comforter and everything else. However, I could never make that connection with my wife Ntombi, although she and my mother Sarah shared important attributes and bonded strongly.

I am grateful that, like my mother, Ntombi has unshakeable principles and is fearless. She is not only careful with money but is a disciplined saver and scours the shops for bargains. She, too, has green fingers and is a demon cook. All these are good things, as my gardening and cooking are often disasters, and I am nervous, dreamy and careless with money. I have tried to express the complexities of our relationship in a haiku.

The broken lock that
only my wife can open
is the most secure

But there were differences. Unlike my mother, Ntombi is physically powerful, holds eccentric opinions, and is capable of violent rages. Sarah was practical and calm, and enjoyed fiction, debating and poetry.

Ntombi is not sentimental or a great lover of poetry, but can direct twenty men to demolish and rebuild a house with not a minute, nail or brick wasted or stolen. She can look at a machine and get it working by adjusting a screw or by cutting a washer out of a piece of rubber.

At a certain point in their most serious arguments, my father Fred would accuse my mother of being middle class. I was recently surprised when someone thought it unusual for the term "middle class" to be used as an insult. Fred's own father was semi-literate and was a painter on the railway. Sarah's father had a tailor's shop, welcomed intellectuals to his supper table, and made suits for the prime minister. My mother would point to Fred's primitive attitude to women, his drinking and other failings. It was class war between two ardent Communists who were romantics and loved arguments.

Ntombi is neither working class nor middle class but is a proud peasant. To be a peasant you must own, or aspire to own, a small farm that produces enough to survive on and even to thrive. This means that she is cut from a different social fabric and, like other peasants, typically resolves arguments through secrecy and stubbornness, supported by deep metaphor, loud gestures, low cunning and sudden violence. It does not matter that she has been denied land through colonialism and patriarchy; that is how she feels, thinks and acts.

Ntombi's dream is to have a piece of land stretching up a hill, with its feet in a river. She knows how to build a house with poles, mud bricks and reeds, which will overlook the fields. At night, the livestock will stay inside a kraal of thornbushes. The family will function as prescribed by a suitably evolved tradition that is connected to the land and to their ancestors. Children will migrate to town, but they will regularly visit and send money to keep the homestead warm and smelling of the fresh dung used to polish the mud floors.

I have met and observed peasants and lived among them in Mozambique and Tanzania, and have never understood why the word "peasant" should be used as an insult. I have great respect for peasants, whom I see as entrepreneurs that own a piece of land. In the new digital, dispersed economy they will thrive if they put solar panels on their roofs and connect to the world wide web.

For Ntombi and Gogo the land is inseparable from the ancestors who inhabit it and with whom they often communicate. Cultivation, gathering, culture and community are inseparable.

Long before that, I read about peasants in fiction and in theories. For years I hunted for the author of a phrase I had once read: "Socialism is the abolition of the village idiot", which I think means ending their isolation. I had forgotten who said it and eventually traced it to Lenin, who also attributed socialism, boringly, to electrification, bookkeeping and local councils.

I now understand that Lenin's factors of development, ironically, work best in capitalist economies – provided they are in clean developmental states that serve connected networks of peasants and other entrepreneurs.

There are already paid tours of thriving gardens on the roofs of office blocks in Johannesburg, some of them using hydroponics. I envisage that in future a drone will carry asparagus to a chef waiting at a restaurant nearby who may have previously imported it from Europe. The modern peasant will help Africa liberate itself from a pattern of trade dating from colonialism.

Apart from Ntombi, the only peasant I have lived with was my grandmother Anna Rubin. She died before I met Ntombi, but I often try to imagine what their relationship would have been like. Not only did they share physical characteristics, but they had similar personalities, values and histories. Like Anna, Ntombi cannot sit still for long. She must be productive in the house or the garden: growing, picking, cooking, preserving, fixing and maintaining.

My comparison of the two peasant women began when Ntombi came across a sixty-year-old Harris tweed dressing gown in a pile of clothes I was about to give away. Genuine Harris tweed is indestructible, thanks to the North Sea weather to which the sheep turn their woolly behinds.

"But this is good work," she said, looking at the stitching on an old shirt of mine that Granny Anna had used to re-line the gown. I told her the history of the gown, and in a spirit of friendly competition Ntombi replaced the lining, which had begun to fray after thirty years.

The next morning, I found Ntombi in an old rocking chair by a window sewing the zip on a broken shopping bag, peeling thread off a large roll, and threading the needle in a stream of African light. Two pairs of glasses were perched on her little nose under a woollen cap. She was in every particular like my grandmother, who sat by a window and sewed when she came to stay for a while with my mother, then in exile in London.

Anna, like Ntombi, was a vegetarian who ate fish and was a strict teetotaller. Ntombi loves to brew, just as she loves to bake. But she does not partake and sneers at a glass of beer. I sometimes tell her that a glass or two might do her, and me, a lot of good. Anna called my father a drunken pig of a gentile, which is how my mother translated her phrase "*goyishe yok*". Both are insulting words for gentiles, with *yok* derived from the massacre of Jews in York in 1190.

My sister Lynn was twelve in 1960 when she witnessed Anna giving my father two brown bags filled with thick-skinned condoms. She told him they were to be given to his Catholic family, to prevent them from breeding like red-haired rabbits. Anna was referring to his Irish mother, who had nine children. Fred was staying with Anna in Johannesburg while facing capital charges at the Treason Trial, and he may have thought that hanging was a better option than living with her.

Ntombi has similar views on birth control and spends hours

on the phone berating her relatives for having sons who have no money but go around impregnating women. The continuation of this social cycle drives her mad. Her last words sometimes are, "Even your bastards are having bastards and their bastards will have bastards."

And, like Anna, Ntombi has mellowed with age, despite being afflicted by extremely painful medical conditions. Anna had one infected kidney and Ntombi has developed arthritis and degeneration of the joints and bones, an increasing number of them now artificial or screwed together.

Granny Anna came to visit while I was staying with my mother and younger sister in London. My father was still in prison in South Africa. I was doing A-levels at a college and had to share a single bed with my girlfriend, whom Anna inspected and must have found fit for breeding. Her mother happened to be a Jewish South African although I do not think Granny Anna knew that; and she was dark-skinned, her father being of South Indian origin. Returning from college, I found a new double bed and she told me, "A boy must enjoy."

Since our children have left home Ntombi has refurbished their rooms with expensive double beds, so that if they are tempted to visit they and their partners can be comfortable.

Granny Anna had violent rages and many strange opinions. One was that children were crawling with harmful germs that needed to be scrubbed away with steaming water. My mother often told us how her mild-mannered father would make desperate efforts to save her and her sisters from being boiled alive.

Another opinion was that breastfeeding and eating meat make children savage. My sister Ruth once told someone that this was the reason she and her children were vegetarians. Her friend pointed out of the window. "Then why are they beating the shit out of my children?" she asked.

Ntombi has a different opinion and breastfed our daughter until she was as round as a pumpkin, but she has strange fancies of her own. She saves every eggshell to crush and spread around in the garden to keep snails away. "The smell and the feel make them think of dead snails. They stay away from my plants."

I once came home and found Ntombi and the gardener holding sledgehammers and looking at the place where our sunken, gloomy scullery had been. Ntombi had seen that the back wall of the kitchen supported nothing and had filled the scullery with its rubble. We now have a long, light and airy kitchen, which she designed and had fitted.

Anna, like Ntombi, was a sufficiently expert builder to direct a team of men. She used her carefully accumulated savings to buy, improve and sell old houses.

Without confiding in me, her spendthrift husband, Ntombi also used her savings for projects, the full extent of which I am only discovering now we are retired. For example, she funded the building of houses for relatives in Kwamteyi, where she grew up. She surprised me one day with the gift of a high-end office suite, inserted into a corner of our bedroom. She paid for our children's higher education, helped purchase our cars for cash, and cleared much of our mortgage.

One comparison gave me a challenge. Our son Sipho introduced Ntombi to smartphones, perhaps because, like me, he was driven mad by her screaming down the landline. It is no coincidence that in isiZulu to make a call is to "hit the wire". I used to shout that they could hear her in KwaZulu-Natal or eSwatini without need of a phone.

For a while now Ntombi has been the centre of a global Facebook and WhatsApp network, with her sensitive fingers on lots of pulses, like a spider feeling its threads. Then, after her meds kick in, she plays games until she can fall asleep in the small hours.

Granny Anna died before smartphones had evolved, but I realise that I own a piece of equivalent tech that she did have, called a samovar. An older cousin who lives in Italy inherited it and wanted to pass it on to me. Ntombi and I went to collect it and spent a wonderful week with him and his wife Rosie.

The samovar is a tall brass device, with an inscription in English dated 1850, saying it was a wedding gift, I assume to Anna's grandmother. You pour burning charcoal down a tube surrounded by water, which begins to boil quite quickly. I imagine a hive of village women buzzing round the samovar, fuelled by sweet black tea. They network and share local and global news and rumours, starting with their husbands and other family members, and they connect with other hives regionally as well as in Moscow, Berlin, Paris and New York. I am sometimes tempted to turn the little brass tap, so I can collect some of the stories that might flow out, just as they would if I plugged into Ntombi's smartphone.

I began to think that the many parallels between Ntombi and Anna must be the work of their respective ancestors. The shades would have their own network and guide their living relatives according to the deals they stitch up. Gogo has connections with my dead parents, and she sometimes burns bitter herbs and calls on them to assist their descendants.

Both Ntombi and Anna were forged in similar historical circumstances, which helps explain why, when Mandela was captured at the Rivonia safe house, all the whites arrested were Jews from Eastern Europe.

Anna and her husband Zelic, my maternal grandparents, came from Lithuania, which was then part of the Russian Empire. As Jews they were denied civil rights, and many were confined to crowded shtetls, much as Ntombi's family were confined to "native reserves" and townships in apartheid South Africa. When there was a famine or political unrest, the Tsar blamed the Jews and sent soldiers to punish them, meaning they were free to rape, kill and plunder. Anna was born in 1888 near Kovna (now Kaunas) and survived a pogrom as a child by hiding in a coffin.

Anna's father Jacob Goodman had served in the Russian army and was given some land to farm. The farm did well, but he and his wife Leba had thirteen children and they opened a bakery to augment their income. When Anna was eleven, Jacob and several other bakers were arrested on the pretext that they made matzos with the blood of murdered Christian children. Their bakeries were seized by corrupt officials.

After years of imprisonment without a trial, my great-grandfather was released on condition he sign up as a soldier again. Jacob became brutalised, a violent religious fanatic and a heavy drinker. While he was in prison, ten of his thirteen children died from poverty, Anna being one of the survivors. She became an atheist and a Young Communist, as she wanted to fight the oppression of women and workers. The police began to harass her.

The family fled to England where they worked in a Leeds sweatshop sewing trousers. Jacob joined the British army, which was short of recruits, and was sent to fight in the Anglo-Boer War and guard concentration camps. In 1905, Leba and her children arrived in Durban. While they survived the journey, there were deaths among their fellow third-class passengers due to sickness from the poor food and conditions on board ship. They took a train to Johannesburg, where Anna, then eighteen, found work in a clothing factory, which is where she met the good-looking Zelic, my grandfather.

Zelic's family were radical free-thinkers and socialists, also from Lithuania, and he and his brothers had taken refuge in South Africa to escape political persecution. Ann and Zelic married and opened a tailor's business, with a workshop in their back garden. Very unusually in colonial South Africa, workers who did the same work got the same wages, regardless of ethnicity or origin.

Anna produced enough food to feed fifteen people every night. Apart from students and workers, visitors included current and future intellectuals and politicians, such as the writer Herman Charles Bosman, Manilal Gandhi, son of Mahatma Gandhi, and Moses Mabhida, a future workers' leader. My mother remembers that Moses was teaching himself to read English and always carried a newspaper and a dictionary with him.

In the 1934 Soviet film *Happiness*, which satirises peasant life before the Revolution, a husband and his wife see that their horse is eating the grass roof of their house. He climbs up, grabs at the horse, and falls off the roof. She shakes her head, then climbs up, gets under the horse, and hoists it on her shoulders.

I am the iconic bumbling husband, and Anna and Ntombi are the strong, competent horse-carriers who take charge and get things done. They expect men to have their weaknesses. Anna told one of my cousins that after her fifth child she invented oral contraception. When her husband wanted sex, she said "No!" She added that if men found relief with women she termed "their piss pots", it was no concern of hers.

And how would Anna and Ntombi have bonded? A clue is provided by an incident I observed on a luxury liner when I was eight or nine years old. One of Anna's surprise projects was to take me and my younger sister Ruth on a cruise up the coast of Mozambique and back. Anna, the Russian peasant, pulled out a wad of money from her savings and paid for a suite of cabins, complete with an on-board maid. We scooted around all over the ship, and Ruth recently told me she remembers having unlimited ice cream.

Granny Anna mostly stayed in the suite with the maid, not trusting the wealthy passengers or feeling comfortable around them. The maid was Maria, a small, humble Portuguese woman. She was from a village, and probably illiterate, although she spoke some English and could communicate with Granny Anna. I saw Granny Anna tense whenever Maria was bullied by her superiors, which was often.

One of the ship's officers, perhaps the purser or his deputy, came to visit us now and again. He would tell us loudly how he admired South Africans because they knew what to do with Communists and blacks, just like the Portuguese government. Anna kept quiet. I did not like what he said, but I felt afraid and also kept quiet.

I remembered that officer almost twenty years later when working as a teacher of English in Lisbon. It was 1977, just three years after a coup toppled the fascist regime that had been in power for fifty years. I was sitting down to soup with my landlady, an air hostess who spoke English. I used a dictionary to help read the headlines of *Diário de Notícias*, one of which announced that another torture chamber belonging to the former security police had been discovered in the area where we lived. I asked my landlady what she thought. "How else are they to get respect and keep order?" was her reply. I kept quiet, afraid of having my throat cut while I slept. Fear and fascism go together like soup and bread.

After she packed for us, and just before the ship docked in Cape Town, Maria went to say goodbye to Granny Anna. She waited until the other staff had left the cabin. They hugged each other and both burst into tears. I was glad and embarrassed at the same time.

Some years ago, outside one of the houses we bought when I got a new job, Ntombi was weeding a strip of lawn. An elderly white couple walking their dog approached her. "We should bring our girl to see how you work," they remarked. "She is too lazy to do much in the garden."

Ntombi thought the woman employed by them was probably middle-aged and worked ten hours a day, six days a week. It is highly unlikely she would get any pension. She was like Ntombi's mother, who spent years caring for a sick woman and bringing up other people's children.

She wiped the sweat from her brow and saw that their little dog was the one that often crapped outside our house. She informed them that she owned the house and that if the dog shat on her grass, she would make them eat it. When I heard the story, I was proud and embarrassed at the same time.

Peasants.

Eight
Gogo speaks

Umendo awuthunyelwa gundwane.
Investigate first before getting married (literally, send a rat ahead to find things out).
– Zulu proverb

I WAS BORN NOMVULA MBELE, in Ekuphumuleni, meaning "a place of rest". My father was Baba Samuel Mbele. My mother was Anna from the Khumalo family, so they called her MaKhumalo.

My grandfather was a Methodist minister who started some congregations. The family had fields and many animals – donkeys for carrying people and things, and cattle, sheep, goats, pigs, chickens, ducks and turkeys; even peacocks. Baba Mbele drove the municipal cart that watered the roads in Ladysmith.

I went to school up to Grade 3. What made me unhappy was to leave school. After my mother died, I had to look after sheep and goats so my brothers could go to school. When the herdboys gave me trouble, I would fight them.

When I was older, I went to Steadville location. Like all young girls, after the death of my mother I went to work. While working in Mavelempini I met Mpiko Lukhele, who would be my husband. I was nineteen. The younger sister proposed him for my husband. When living with him, I fell pregnant with Thembalihle and the cheating began. She died two months after she was born.

It was when I lived in Kwamteyi that I became the slave of the family. My family was far away, on the other side of Ladysmith.

Ntombi was born and was very sick. The healer pretended to bury her sister instead of Ntombi, telling the ancestors she was a twin to her dead sister Thembalihle. That trick allowed Ntombi to live.

After Ntombi there was a boy, Sifiso, who died at childbirth and was buried in a safe place in Ekuphumuleni. Then Khumbulani was born. He was a happy child until he saw he had no father figure.

The Lukhele family took Ntombi and Khumbulani away from me to Swaziland. I told my family how I was very sad and depressed to lose them. I went to work for a family in Ladysmith. The husband worked and was very strict. The pay was little – in 1993 I got R150 a month only. They were also kind, especially the wife and children, who helped dress my children.

I was scared to get on the plane for the first time to Cape Town. When I was there, I missed my sisters a lot. I was very happy to meet my daughter. And happy to meet the husband John and Busi and Fred and Sarah.

When I saw John, I thought he looked like the son of the white family I had worked for. John is the best son I ever wanted. Sarah was a kind woman who took care of her family until the end. It was the same with Fred. The Carneson girls have a strong bond with my daughter. They give me hugs and kisses. Very friendly.

Busi and Sipho spoil me: send me for massages on my birthday and give gifts. I worried about them finding jobs.

Now I worry about my strength and health as I am getting frail.

Translated from isiZulu by Ntombi

Nine
The bed that was never mine

Cry "Havoc!" and let slip the dogs of war,
That this foul deed shall smell above the earth
With carrion men, groaning for burial.
– William Shakespeare, *Julius Caesar*, Act 3, Scene 1

UNLIKE MY FATHER AND NTOMBI, I was never part of the army of the ANC, Umkhonto we Sizwe, so I never was a dog of war. But the apartheid security machine did not differentiate. As active opponents of apartheid and members of the ANC, we were among the prey they hunted and drove into exile – a condition that unleashes its own kind of emotions and realities.

Visiting other countries does broaden your mind, but that depends on your state of mind. In a strange land, where you do not speak the language, you view things as reflections of a reality you can only partially know.

If you have been in this situation, then you probably stopped for coffee in a roadside café or in a railway station. You view and hear everything through a dusty plate-glass window. To establish if your train has arrived, you peer through reflections of the lights at the people, and try to catch distorted announcements in a foreign language. Among the reflections and the babble of sounds, you begin to form a dim picture of what is going on.

Prejudices are confirmed through a refraction process, whereby you focus the little light that you have, using lenses and other devices you have brought with you. You might observe two soldiers quarrelling loudly and assume they must be discussing politics because you read somewhere that a coup is in the air. Every machine in the café may appear dated or broken, and a visitor might assume that the country is heading for a recession, with development held back by corruption.

The more objective reality is that one soldier probably owes the other money; and the café is run-down because hardly anyone uses trains anymore, preferring cars or buses.

Both exiles and tourists experience such perceptual distortions, but their situations are quite different. Ntombi and I have visited six countries as tourists since we returned to South Africa from exile in 1993. The first thing we noticed was that our new South African passports elicited a completely different response from the dubious travel documents we used when we were in exile. Before our return in 1993 we had to pretend to be relaxed when our documents produced sour looks on the faces of immigration officers.

The poet Vladimir Mayakovsky gave expression to this. "My new Soviet passport", he wrote in a poem in the 1920s, "shall gnaw through red tape like a wolf." He was never in exile but travelled abroad after his poetry became popular and before he killed himself. Perhaps Comrade Stalin depressed him. He liked Mayakovsky's poetry but thought him unreliable – often a prelude to his having someone rubbed out of life, books and even history.

The second thing we noticed was that as tourists with dollars or euros we had a different relationship with our host countries and their people. An exile asks to be given protection for an indefinite length of time. She or he may come with skills but also with few resources and many problems.

After a period of exile in Tanzania, many South Africans reached a point where they felt trapped and began to think of possible lives they could lead elsewhere. This was a feeling that was typical of exiles. That time arrived for me in 1986. There were two routes open to most of us: recruitment to Umkhonto we Sizwe, via military training in Angola, or a scholarship to study abroad. I began to haunt the scholarship office, run by two efficient Mazimbu-grown bureaucrats. Like other applicants, I caught "scholarship fever" and became increasingly neurotic and agitated.

I could not imagine being separated from Ntombi and our toddler Busi. Ntombi supported my plans, provided we go as a family to connect with the other Carnesons – my mother, father and two sisters – who were in exile in London.

The scholarship office found Ntombi a funder who would support her and pay for her chef training at Southgate, the London college where I had done well at my A-levels. More than ten years had passed, but I remembered the teachers who had inspired me. I was accepted by the Institute of Education in London to do a master's in curriculum development and also secured a scholarship. My parents declared they would host us, and we applied for visas.

One of the symptoms of scholarship fever was that in the final stages you developed a phobia against Mazimbu. Although we were warned about possible visa problems, our courses were about to start, and we went to wait in Dar es Salaam.

The Britain I remembered was that of the exile community and the people who were active in the anti-apartheid movement. I thus had no idea that under Thatcher we were classed as terrorists and our visa request was grinding through the fine-toothed cogs of the British security system.

We waited over a month, and in that time Busi was attacked by malaria, despite all our efforts to protect her. We experienced the kind of powerlessness and fear that are only experienced by exiles. We were staying at the YMCA and had no way of communicating with the ANC at night, no transport or knowledge of the health system, and little money. Our baby's temperature soared and we asked a taxi driver to take us to the nearest hospital. The driver was concerned and helpful and took us to the Agha Khan, one of the hospitals around the world donated by the stateless religious leader. Busi received expert, free treatment and survived, and we will always be grateful for that.

We finally got our visas for the UK and boarded an Air Ethiopia plane, bound for London. The stewardesses spoiled Busi outrageously as she bounced around the plane. We settled into my parents' small suburban house in North London, which we shared with them for almost a year. We both studied, while they looked after Busi, who began attending a nursery school. I had to lay down boards in the attic to make a floor, where I created a study, accessed by climbing a ladder. It was freezing in winter and an oven in summer.

My assumption was that, culturally, Ntombi would be the one at a disadvantage and would gratefully rely on me as a guide to the English, on whom I considered myself an authority. I had survived for three years at an English private school,[5] and then six more years at a technical college and university. Much of my childhood was spent immersed in English literature. But assumptions are often misleading, as I was to learn.

In London we hardly met an English person socially. Busi's first best friend was the daughter of a Swiss woman whom we met when pushing our toddler around a park. She was married to an exiled Iranian. Their child spoke only German to her mother, Farsi to her father, and English to us. We mainly interacted with English natives with whom we worked or studied, or who kept shops, were bus conductors or drove taxis.

I had told Ntombi about the tribe known as Cockneys so she could more fully understand and enjoy *East Enders* with my parents. It was essentially a family drama, and Ntombi worked out all the issues and relationships long before I did.

The first live Cockney she met was the driver of a black cab, which was transporting us and Busi's pushchair. I farted and was about to blame Busi when the cabbie turned around and said, "Someone is baking mince pies." Ntombi enthusiastically replied by giving him her favourite recipe for mince pies. The cabbie and I started laughing, and Ntombi's face grew dark and murderous. I tried to explain what was amusing about the situation, but even now, when I try to tell the story, she says she will never forgive me "or that driver, the other white racist". Given the everyday racism black people in Britain had to endure, her anger at our response was and is fully justified.

However, I began to worry that Ntombi might soon face an assault charge when she reported that a bus conductor said, "Can I see your ticket, luv." She told me that she had replied loudly that she was not and would never be his love. She adapted soon after I explained the term, and now regularly calls me "love".

Ntombi did ask me about things that looked interesting but that she could not quite understand. One example was a story that appeared nightly on the news, about the owner of a London brothel, who called herself Madame Whiplash. She had formed a political party and had sued the state for taxing her, arguing that it was living on immoral earnings. One day, she waved a little black book at the cameras and claimed that it contained the names of all her clients, including half the cabinet and senior Tory backbenchers.

Ntombi demanded to know what it was all about. When I said that some men paid large sums to be whipped, Ntombi's eyes widened. She asked me to write to the Madame, saying that we would join her party and that she would volunteer to thrash all the bad men. I was tempted to tell Ntombi she might be appointed Chief Whip of the party, but she may have taken my joke seriously.

I completed my MA on curriculum development, gaining a distinction, and then worked for a year visiting primary and high schools to teach immigrant children English. I remember one child refugee from Afghanistan, who looked up at me with his large dark eyes and recited, "My name is Abdul. Teach me English." Ntombi was studying and doing well at her college, academically and socially.

My confidence in being a reliable guide to English society was put to the test when I went back to being a full-time classroom teacher. I was appointed to teach nine-year-olds in an inner-city school in Tottenham, not far from the football club. We rented a flat in a busy road that was a walk away from the school, across a park. Ntombi took Busi to a preschool class there and also collected her. The staff and the pupils were welcoming and supportive.

Four learners from my class of nine-year-olds remain in my accessible memory. These characters were a Leftish Lawyer, and a small Fearless Girl we all respected because she was quick, honest and tough. Then there were two that I now realise had special needs: an illiterate and therefore frustrated Disruptor; and a slow-learning and gentle Black Child whom the Disruptor picked on. I took them for all subjects.

During the first break the Lawyer sidled up to me and said, "Bloody Thatcher. If it weren't for her, I would be downing a nice quarter-pint of milk." Not knowing the protocols for discussing politics with nine-year-olds, I smiled and said nothing.

His suspicions about me were confirmed when I introduced them to a daily BBC performance of *The Wind in the Willows*, having found a tape in a cupboard. He approached me again. "You know that story you play on the tape every day? How come the good guys sound posh like you, and the nasty little villains, the toe-rags, all sound like us?" I agreed that he had a point and advised him to write to the BBC.

I eventually asked about the Disruptor's inability to read and was told his mum had once taken him to a specialist, but nothing had come of it. His mother was worried and protective and put pressure on me when I complained about his violent and disruptive behaviour. I paid much less attention to the slow learner, because it was a large class and his charming and better-educated West Indian mother was nice to me. I did attempt to protect her child from being abused by the Disruptor and tried to encourage him.

Some projects were magical. I would initiate a project and the class then took ownership and ran with it. One day I found two kilos of tiny glass beads in a bag at the back of a cupboard, filled a large jar with them, and challenged the class to count them. The winning team invented their own system of measuring volume and constructed standard containers and a sensitive balance to weigh the beads. For weeks I went home with tiny beads in my hair and clothes.

My biggest fear was PE class in the gym, as I am not sporty and had received no training when doing my postgraduate teacher's certificate in 1975. I improvised some games that the class adopted enthusiastically and creatively. One involved asking them to stick bits of cloth in their shorts to make a tail, with the winner collecting the most tails. These games only soaked up a fraction of their energy. One day the mood changed, and I realised they knew that I did not know what I was doing.

The Disruptor leapt on to the Black Child and began beating him. I panicked, grabbed him by the back of the neck, and hauled him off roughly. He ran out crying, saying he would tell his mum. She later confronted me in my classroom. She was tall and fit, and I watched her right hand, expecting a slap or a roundhouse punch. She got me with a straight left to the jaw. I stayed upright and continued teaching. She stormed into the principal's office and laid a complaint.

My world imploded. I was told to stay at home until procedures had been followed. As an exile I was highly vulnerable. I knew nothing about the system, had no support network, and foolishly had not joined a union. If I lost the job, I would not be able to provide for my family and, if not granted refugee status, we could be deported, possibly back to South Africa.

I do not deal with failure well, and I thought that my work and my relationship with the class and the staff were as ashes, and that my worth on earth and claim to a profession were destroyed.

The principal was exceptionally able, and three days later I was back teaching the class, having apologised in writing and verbally. He told me such incidents were common, but I knew that I had to find a way of helping the Disruptor to learn and to build his self-respect – and, thus, regain mine.

Ntombi finished the second year of her chef training course, which was City and Guilds, an internationally recognised certificate. She passed with the highest second-year marks and was awarded a prize. After she graduated, she found herself at home in a small flat with no garden, no job and a five-year-old Busi who spent half the day in preschool. A Ntombi who is not busy and productive does not exist. She began perfecting her sugar craft, using marzipan which she coloured with dyes to make wonderfully decorated cakes, for my family and for the ANC.

A week after the incident with the Disruptor, Ntombi was in my class, teaching them the basic skills of sugar craft. We supplied the marzipan, dyes, brushes and the paper plates to construct their flowers on. Without being obvious, she paid special attention to the Disruptor, who was transformed. He was by far the most focused and disciplined learner and produced the best work.

All previous tasks I had set him had an element of reading, and he could not make sense of the jumble of shapes we see as letters. I had not heard of the affliction known as dyslexia and apparently none of the other staff had either.

I taught competently enough, but something had broken and the magic for me had gone. What was clear was that something was wrong with me and with the school system and curriculum.

Before we left, the principal brought me a message from the mother of the Disruptor, who was making progress – she who had fought like a lioness for her child. She thanked Ntombi for her help. The principal said that I must tell my wife that they had varnished the sugar flowers, glued them to a board, had the board framed and hung on their living-room wall.

The learner I describe as the Leftish Lawyer indicated that I had social dyslexia. This took the form of blindness to the culture and actual situation of the working class, which was not the case with the principal and many of the teachers. They remained close to their roots. He suspected me of being a blinkered and biased member of the middle class, and it did not matter that my head was full of ideologies and theories about society.

What convinced me that the child lawyer's suspicions were well founded was the relationship I had with the working-class family who lived opposite us in the small block of flats in Tottenham to which we had moved. I now realise that I never knew their surname, and I cannot remember any of their names. To write about my views and experience, I have had to rely on the memory of Ntombi, who does not suffer from class dyslexia and who had a solid relationship with the family.

Let us call the family the Smiths. Frank, the father, and Kate, the mother, were in their thirties and had the health, vigour, charm and ravishing good looks of Cockneys portrayed in films. They were an exceptionally cheerful and friendly family. I sometimes caught glimpses of Frank through his doorway, with his shirt off and Kate trying to get tar out of his skin and hair. The baby was often entangled with a lively puppy. Frank's work was laying roofing and he was often away from home. Cathy, the oldest child, perhaps nine or ten, adopted us and was serious and responsible.

I was home in the late afternoon and on weekends, and often joined them for walks in the park. Cathy pushed the baby in a pram and her brother of six or seven followed behind with Busi, who climbed into her pushchair when tired. When I was at work, they came to play with Busi, who went in and out of the two flats. Their mother was friendly with Ntombi, who reminded me years later that she was given a parcel of Cathy's outgrown clothes. I can remember the golden teddy-bear designs on the warm flannel pyjamas.

It was on one of these walks that Cathy proudly informed me that the puppy was a pitbull. I had read accounts in the paper of savage attacks by pitbulls, who experts said were dangerous and unpredictable. I asked Cathy if the puppy was safe, and she told me the dog was well cared for. I explained that I meant safe to be around children. Cathy was puzzled, then gave me the same suspicious look I had seen on the face of the child lawyer. I tried to hide my fear but revealed it every time Busi went into their flat.

I enjoyed reading to Busi and found an illustrated poem in an

Oxfam shop that we both loved: *Lizzy's Lion* by Dennis Lee and Marie-Louise Gay. I still remember the first and last verses:

> Lizzy had a lion
> With a big bad roar
> And she kept him the bedroom
> By the closet-cupboard door.

***

> (One night a "rotten robber with a rotten robber's mask" broke in, and the inevitable happened.)

***

> Then old Lizzy and her lion
> Took the toes & tum and head,
> And they put them in the garbage,
> And they both went back to bed.

I read it to both children and asked Cathy if she wanted to borrow it. For the first time I saw her upset and angry, "I hate this book. My father does robberies." I apologised and promised to put the book away, but I knew I had been identified as being one of Them.

Reflecting on exile and the cold and hot wars we lived through, and the half-finished revolutions we are still living through, I feel rage, despair and not much hope. What I cannot control are events that catch me by surprise and cause an emotion or memory to be released from wherever it is caged in my head.

For example, just before the Covid lockdown a friend who is an MK veteran told me he had made friends with a veteran of the apartheid army. They had fought on opposite sides in Angola. His friend had written a memoir, which he lent me. The friend had returned to Cuito Cuanavale, where a decisive battle had raged. He then cycled back to South Africa, engaging with people on the way. His account is honest and moving.

I then read another memoir, written by another ageing white South African who suffers from memories of the war against

SWAPO in Namibia. He was a teenager then and he still finds it amusing that an older soldier used the naked body of a Namibian woman they had killed to give young soldiers a sex lesson. My rage was such that I later discovered that a tiny blood vessel in one eye had burst. I said aloud that if I were the child or grandchild of that woman I would not rest until I found the author and confronted him. The same applies to the editor, publisher and others who saw nothing wrong with the text because of how they still think, feel and write about black people.

Then I thought of how Ntombi might react. She had risked and suffered far more than I had. Before retiring, Ntombi had been an officer in the new army and had chosen to work closely with white soldiers who were racist and who had fought against the ANC. She liked their skills and work ethics and shared many values with them. If she had overheard one of them telling the same story, she would have talked with him until he could picture his own mother lying naked and someone violating her corpse, and built from there.

I remember being in exile in London when my father joined us after his release from prison. I would hear about some terrible atrocity being committed and would tell him that we should reply with a war that would "make ash-monuments of their children", quoting a line in a poem by Mazisi Kunene.

"I was never in the struggle for revenge," he would reply, shaking his head sadly.

Ten

The Dark Chef and the ethnographer

In order for ethnology to live, its object must die; by dying, the object takes its revenge for being "discovered" and with its death defies the science that wants to grasp it.
– Jean Baudrillard, *Simulacra and Simulation,* 1983

When we were in exile, I gave notice at the London primary school where I was teaching, informing the principal that I had been offered a doctoral research post at the University of Sunderland. We gave our landlord notice and I phoned around for information about the town we would be moving to. It had a reputation for being rough and racist, and I asked a colleague what he knew about it. He said, "The barmaids are rumoured to eat their young."

This cryptic statement made more sense after learning about Sunderland from my sister Ruth, who informed me that she had lived there for a few months with her then partner. I will call him Sid, which is not his real name. She told me of an encounter between Sid and a shaven ex-soldier outside a pub he had just left. The former soldier had been giving him the hard eye because Sid was dark, being of Turkish stock, and hairy, being a free spirit.

He was unlocking his bicycle when the man threatened him, and a frightened Sid swung the chain and hit the man's temple with a heavy padlock. The man shook his head and said, "Now I'm going to kill you," and went to his car to fetch weapons. Sid rushed back to the bar and called friends, who escorted him and his bicycle home to Ruth. He was later told that the man was mentally ill and had been dismissed from the army for being too violent.

This story gave me pause for thought. Teaching and living in an inner-city London school had taught me that I was not good at relating to working-class communities and individuals living outside books.

Then there was the racism. Ntombi and our preschool child Busi might be physically harmed and, being small and unarmed, I might not be able to protect them. We would be several hours' drive away from London, where we had family and friends who were connected to anti-apartheid and anti-racist networks.

Sunderland sits astride the mouth of the River Wear and was famous in its day for its coal mining and ship building. Over the bridge from the old town there are large council housing estates, which is where I rented a house through an agency.

Our bus driver landlord met us with the keys and smiled at Ntombi, saying, "No offence, pet, but we like to say that we don't stop for Scotsmen, niggers or dogs." Ntombi only took offence at the word "pet", which she associated with the word "dog", used in many Zulu insults. The Zulu song I sing and dance to best has the chorus "Izinja, zobolani lezo izinja". They (the whites) are dogs, we will kill them like dogs. I suspect the song is sung to smiling tourists when gold miners do gumboot dances for them.

Ntombi told me afterwards, her anger growing, "I am not his pet." I explained that it was a term of endearment probably derived from petal and applied to all human females, except perhaps royalty.

While I was nervous walking around Sunderland, Ntombi liked the look and feel of the rough, working-class town. She began going over the bridge into town to seek work. On the first day she was enticed into an office by Scientologists who offered to test her and find her employment. When I explained their real mission, I had to prevent Ntombi from finding an iron bar and testing it on their heads. Her response surprised and alarmed me, although it was exactly what some locals would have done.

The administrative staff at the School of Education were horrified when they were told we were living over the river in the notorious housing estates. They spoke of cars on bricks, decaying apartment blocks full of unmarried mums, broken windows, and toddlers with filthy nappies around their knees. I tried to explain that the house we rented was at the posh end of the estate, where Thatcher had encouraged the council to sell off council houses and people had done them up, but their prejudice ran deep.

I decided to do my doctoral research on understanding classroom practice in a high school and two primary schools in the same housing estates. Applied ethnography would be used to study the natives in their habitat, just as British anthropologists had studied Ntombi and her kin in the colonies.

I shadowed six teachers and helped them out while I observed and scribbled notes, following a cohort of kids from primary to high school. At night I typed up and wove together hundreds of story threads. I tracked themes and arrived at some conclusions. I still suffer from the arthritis that began with my thesis, as I actually wore my fingers to the bone.

It made no sense to continue renting, and we put down a deposit for a cottage that was for sale in the old town. All the cottages in the short street were the same, two up and two down and joined at the hip, front door on the street and a brick yard behind, what the Portuguese call *en comboio*, as if each house is a railway carriage.

In London, we could barely survive on my schoolteacher's salary.

In Sunderland I earned about half as much, but we could own a car and a cottage. I had been advised to get the car from a teacher who did them up, and discovered too late that he worked on written-off cars. The chassis was as bent as the teacher, someone explained when I complained about the tyres wearing out on one side. I learned that you must keep your wits sharp when doing business in Sunderland. I had been in London too long, growing soft and denying myself the education that comes from mixing socially with workers.

Respectable lower middle-class and middle to upper working-class families had lived in our cottage from Victorian times. Before they squeezed bathrooms into the cottages, people used an outhouse and a tap in the little brick yard. When I drilled into a wall, I discovered the cottage had six layers of skin in the form of wallpaper, with at least one a William Morris.

There was hardly any traffic and the kids played in the cobbled street, going into one another's houses. Busi graduated to a primary school that was round the corner, and several families had adopted us by the end of the first week. It was the kind of community that was dying across Britain. Families had been moved from street-based communities to massive housing estates such as the ones across the river.

I usually live for my work and among my books, oblivious of my surroundings. Within a week of moving into the cottage, Ntombi knew what was going on. One or two families that were hard up borrowed items like sugar and soap regularly; Ntombi also came from communities that survived through human solidarity. In our little street I was able to experience this for myself and found there was a price to pay. Ntombi knew in detail why the families were hard up, and so did the rest of the neighbours. Judgements and opinions were whispered among the wives and the men in the pub at the end of the street.

As our first Christmas in Sunderland approached, I was gathered up by the menfolk and taken to the pub. "Why is the place so quiet?" one asked as we sat down. Someone nodded at a table in the corner where card games were being played. "A woman came in earlier, having heard that her husband had lost all their holiday money. Kids had looked forward to it for months. She screamed at him for five minutes and turned over the table."

All the men around me looked penitent and hung their heads for a moment. They perked up and began on the serious business of the evening, to get this dozy young foreigner pissed as a newt. After they carried me home, a disgusted Ntombi instructed Busi to carry buckets to her father and empty the vomit in the toilet. "Daddy's drunk!" she shouted now and again, splitting my head open.

My parents visited us, and we have a photograph of the five of us standing on the paving in the tiny yard, and it shows Busi smiling through the gap where her two front teeth were to grow. Her eyes are squeezed tight from the effort. My father is standing in a military at-ease position with a button-up cardigan straining to cover a round tummy. He had been released from prison in South Africa a few years before, and his eyes remained still full of pain that never quite went away. Sarah is smiling. She had been spoiled by a tired Ntombi, who has an Afro and had cooked up a storm for her in-laws. I have a heavy beard and a much flatter tummy.

Most Sunderland folk were friendly and welcoming, but more than once a group of racist youths shouted "Paki" at Ntombi. She could not understand how they mistook her for someone from Pakistan. I explained that they had adopted the word as an insult for all people of colour, and most had a very weak grasp of geography.

A student from Kenya told me how she and her friends were celebrating the award of her PhD in an Italian restaurant. They had a table by the window, and for ten minutes a group of youths leapt up and down on the pavement, gibbering to indicate that the students were monkeys.

I wrote an angry letter to the Dean of Students, threatening to write to all African ambassadors, telling them their students would not be safe in Sunderland. Students lived off campus in town, and I demanded that they speak to the Sunderland town council and do something to combat racism. Some weeks later a few anti-racist posters were put up around town.

With her catering qualifications and experience, Ntombi got a job at a government old-age home. Her schedule allowed her to do a specialist part-time course in patisserie at South Shields, halfway to Newcastle. The college had a nursery school where she could leave Busi while attending class.

Very soon the old folk began to ask for more cooking to be done by the lady they called the Dark Chef. Ntombi was popular for several reasons. The meat they were usually given was far too tough for them to chew, partly because some members of staff liked to take leftover meat home. Ntombi braised it for an hour until it fell apart, adding herbs and spices which she asked the management to buy. "I put the client first, always," she told them.

She began to improve dishes like pease pudding, a kind of mash made from crushed peas; and they even preferred her Yorkshire pudding and roasts. Lastly, she baked cookies and tarts for the old folks' visitors, which brought their relatives and friends around more often. She kept an eye on the pensioners' property, advising them to hide valuables away when the cleaners or relatives were due to come round.

Back home she began making soup out of fish heads which she got fresh at a fish market. She walked there with one of the neighbours. The locals told her that to their knowledge nobody had made that before, and a few asked for the recipe. The trick, which I have never mastered, is to boil them just long enough. The stock will be bitter if the fish bones in the mix are boiled for too long.

My background research confirmed my observations, that the working class had well-defined and mutually hostile sub-classes. Where we lived in our cottage, there were norms that distinguished us from the lower orders across the river. Ntombi was told by several women that it was not nice to carry home shopping in bags from the cheapest supermarket. She was advised, when shopping in cheap shops, to transfer the items to bags from Marks and Spencer.

Another finding from my research over the river was that any middle-class people entering the housing estates were regarded as the enemy, whether police officer, politician, priest, teacher or social worker. Not one teacher at the schools lived in the area. A high school kid told me the "Polis kilt my best mate. They chased him and he war just twokking." This translates as: his best friend had a fatal accident because the police gave chase after he Took a Vehicle Without Consent for a joy ride.

Apart from selling off state assets and making dentists rich by stopping free school milk, Thatcher had run-ins with the unions led by the strong coal miners. Ntombi likes strong leaders and fancied one of them, Arthur Scargill. She also liked the fiery speeches of Dennis Skinner, a Labour backbencher whom the press called the Beast of Bolsover.

Thatcher imported cheap coal from Poland. This helped to destroy one of the industries that had supported communities known for having unbreakable unions and for voting Labour. The last two coal mines in Sunderland were scheduled to close. We were friendly with a miner and his wife, and Busi played with their daughter. Ntombi helped his wife get a job at the old-age home.

One day, I decided to walk across the bridge rather than take the bus. The sky was blue, and the seagulls were noisy but kept a respectful distance. They were known locally as shite hawks and liked to humble people who were overdressed. I stopped to look at tugs pulling a huge ferry down the River Wear towards the sea. A passing local told me, "That is the last ship. The shipyards are aboot to close doon. Half of all English ships were built he-are over the past two hundred years." He called the river We-are, rather than Wear.

At a school the next morning, a beaming child came up to me in the playground and said with pride, "Me mam's boyfriend got a job at Nissan." The Japanese had built a giant car factory outside the town and were very picky about any locals they employed. If they were accepted for an interview, they were given three separate tests.

A boy interrupted and asked, "What happened to the Avon lady?" I had no idea what that meant but worked it out when he said, "Max Factor." The teacher whom I was shadowing rescued me. "Stop clartin' aboot," she told him in the vernacular. "Clarts are what come from the backend of cows," she explained in the Queen's English. I made a note about code-switching, starting another theme I would track across the sample.

Some of my findings supported the neo-Marxist theories of Bowles and Gintis, who held that the fragmentation of the school curricula served to control knowledge. I collected drawings that the primary school kids did of electric circuits they had worked on during class projects. They were better than similar drawings done by learners during a thirty-minute science class in their second year of secondary school. English primary school learners were behind their German or Japanese peers in maths and science, but researchers at the time found they were better at projects and creative problem-solving.

A marvellous primary schoolteacher I observed had been a CEO of a company when he suddenly got the calling. One day I casually asked him what he thought of the affable and friendly principal. His head whipped round and there was a hint of fear in his eyes. "How long would I have to work here full-time to understand that glance?" I asked him. He told me about six months, and I realised that applied ethnography was easier to read about than to do.

Somewhere in my garage, after all these years, is a video tape I took of this teacher on an obsolete mini-cassette. His class was performing a Christmas play. It was a satire on the way he organised projects in his classroom, using his business skills. He hinted that this was the source of tension with the principal, who favoured more conventional teaching methods.

The children loved their teacher, but they had to perform tasks according to his card system, which became increasingly complex and a brake on their creativity. They were dressed as dwarves, working in a Task Mine, and carried huge sacks labelled tasks.

"Task, task, task," they chanted as they trudged around the stage.

We began to be woven into the lives of some of the families in the street where we lived – a different situation from London, where we hardly met the English socially except at work or at college or while engaged in anti-apartheid activities. Our lives in London were centred in the South African émigré community. I looked up the meaning of "émigré" in *Lexico* and I realised that is precisely what we felt like when we lived in London:

> Émigré [ˈeməˌɡrā]: a person who has left their own country to settle in another, typically for political reasons. SYNONYMS: stranger, visitor, non-member, odd man out, foreigner, alien, outlander, immigrant, emigrant, incomer, newcomer, parvenu, arriviste, interloper, intruder, gatecrasher, outcast, misfit, individualist, nonconformist, free spirit, unorthodox person, original, bohemian, eccentric, maverick, rebel, dissenter, dissident.

In general, I felt welcomed in Sunderland, but not in London, even after living there on and off for ten years. This was one reason why I could never bring myself to apply for British citizenship, unlike the rest of my family and most resident exiles. Defenders of apartheid were suspicious of holders of dual citizenship, who they called *soutpiele* – salty penises – as they had one foot in South Africa and one elsewhere, with their *piele* dangling in the sea.

The main reason, however, is that I am, as Ntombi often points out, a dreamer who is impractical, with romantic illusions about the struggle – and who, because of this, puts work first instead of the family and things like a convenient second nationality.

I shared a dusty office in a converted attic of the education faculty with several other research assistants doing degrees. I remember Patrick, Paula and Mike. We became good friends, and Ntombi sometimes talks about them still. Patrick made us welcome in his home, as did my long-suffering tutor.

Paula was very bright, tough and working class. Mike was

what my mother would call a *mensch* in Yiddish – a regular guy, in American. He loved running over hills and moors, despite a dicky heart; and he wanted his ashes scattered over the grounds of Sunderland football cub. He took me to see Sunderland playing at home against a London team, the first professional game I ever watched standing up. When I asked him why we did not sit down, he patiently explained, "No other way to feel the game." He would never say so, but I had betrayed my class orientation by wanting to be seated.

Months later I made the mistake of catching the train to nearby Newcastle on the day they were playing Sunderland. A crowd of supporters disembarked, their war cries echoing around the station. The Newcastle supporters were waiting for them, howling death threats. I was in the middle, together with a few policemen standing in a row. I instantly understood and appreciated the phrase "the thin blue line", and realised that my instincts remained solidly middle class.

My tutor and boss – a tolerant and progressive intellectual – would not have been impressed with the level of our office conversations in the attic. Trying to open a window, I would ask, "Is it safe? We may get some new ideas flying into the room," to which Mike would always reply, "Keep it closed – the few ideas we have might escape." Having opened it a crack, I would make a cup of tea and say I would try to throw the bag out of the window from my desk. Paula had a thing about tea bags. I would ask, "What if I miss and it slides down the pane?" She replied, dead serious, "The world would not be big enough to hide yourself in."

The rough tongue and sharp mind of Paula kept me focused, academically and politically. We were obliged to attend a talk by a visiting speaker on some abstruse aspect of school curricula. After forty minutes I whispered to her that it must be pleasant to be a gentleman academic, flitting hither and yon over fields of knowledge. "Oh, you mean a wanker," she replied loudly.

Eleven

The Beast and Aunty Bella's cabinet

Prejudice is a burden that confuses the past, threatens the future and renders the present inaccessible.
– Maya Angelou, *All God's Children Need Travelling Shoes*, 1986

We returned to South Africa towards the end of 1993, assisted by the International Organization of Migration and the United Nations. I rushed through the process in a daze. This was partly because of excitement and the job I had lined up at the University of Cape Town; and partly because of my nervousness about the apartheid Beast, which was very much alive and might sink its teeth into us. I was especially afraid of how we would deal with racist abuse and protect our daughter. We knew there was state-sponsored political violence and high levels of crime.

Ntombi took a practical view and complained bitterly when we sold our cottage and car cheaply and left a lot of our household goods behind in England. Twenty-five years later she still has not forgiven me. "You were full of your work at the university, with that little pay so we could not buy anything. You thought you would be a someone when you came back. I had to bake with a pot covered by a plate and hunt like a cat in the night for things in second-hand shops."

Thanks to Ntombi's money management skills and help from my parents, we had enough savings to put down a deposit for a house and a used car. Most important, Ntombi's mother Nomvula came to stay in 1994, a few months before the birth of our son Sipho in December. Her assistance with Sipho and housework allowed Ntombi to get a job. She also provided crucial moral support, especially for Ntombi, trapped in a white, suburban world.

At the time I was only vaguely aware of the value of Ntombi and her mother, and certainly did not appreciate them enough. Nor was I engaged enough with my children, and my largest regret is not remembering about their childhoods in South Africa. I can recall only a few episodes from the time of our return, such as the birthdays held in Kirstenbosch Botanical Gardens or school projects I helped with.

Trying to look back into memories that are still clouded by anxiety and fears, I remember there was love, but there was also a mountain of neglect that I must atone for. Fear of the Beast played a part, but the underlying reason was that after returning to my homeland I contracted a hidden but serious disease that would blight our lives. The common name for this sickness is workaholism, which is like its boozy cousin, with addiction to stress replacing the evils of alcohol.

There were many kinds of anxiety. We stayed for a while with Fred and Sarah in their suburban flat, and the day after our arrival I had to go into the city centre to claim my newly deracialised South African identity document. The newspapers were full of stories about criminals and groups armed by the state attacking people on trains. I decided to take a minibus taxi into Cape Town. I had left South Africa in 1966 when such taxis never entered the white suburbs and public transport was provided by municipal buses.

There I was, a white among coloured and African passengers who offered me advice in Afrikaans, which I hardly understood. As a boy I used to take the same route to school in a racially segregated bus, and would stare into District Six. This was a spirited ghetto from which the mostly coloured community was later expelled when the area was declared white. On my return I was flooded with emotions and memories. As a child I always used to marvel at the defiant sentence painted across a cracked white wall in District Six: "Welcome to Fairy Land".

Just before I got off, near the City Hall, a man walked in front of the bus and the driver swore at him. The man swore back, comparing, in rhythmic and poetic Afrikaans, the driver's mother to a baboon's anus worn out from being over-used. The driver got out and chased the man up the road. It was a magic moment, and my fears were temporarily forgotten. I finally felt at home.

The Beast of racism and colonialism showed its face to me a week later. I was collecting my daughter at the same primary school I had attended, once strictly for whites only. She came up to the car, looking disturbed and said, "You are white, mum is black, and I am coloured." My heart broke, and I deeply regret not knowing what to say.

I had begun working at the university, and the next day I was late and had to go and look for Busi in the playground. There were lots of children around, but all the black and coloured children were in the sandpit, not talking and not playing. They were refugees from the currents and eddies of racism that washed through the school: a look here and a whisper there; the teachers' eyes on them. I felt a violent surge of emotions but still could not say anything to Busi, who was subdued rather than her normal buzzing self.

Another bite of the Beast, which hurts us until now, is the way Ntombi was treated by one of my father's aunts and some members of her family. My father had been largely cut off from his family since the 1950s by class, race, and his being at war with the apartheid regime. Geography was also a factor, as his family lived far away in Natal and the Transvaal.

Being middle class and caught up in the same war, and with most of the white working class being deeply racist, I was hardly aware of the emotional strain on my father. Nor did I ever think of his mother and father as my grandparents. I once had a glimpse of a thin woman, in a photo he kept somewhere, who I assumed was his mother. After his release from prison and when we were living in exile together in London, he received a letter saying she had died. He lay on his bed and quietly cried, and nobody comforted him. The memory still fills me with shame and regret.

Ntombi is not middle class in terms of culture or thinking and is completely family centred. My lack of reaction to the death of my paternal grandmother would have shocked her, and she would have immediately consoled my father.

Now back in Cape Town, my father told us that his older sister Bella was living in an old-age home in the city and was very frail. Ntombi immediately wanted to go to her and show respect for her as an elder of the family and give her comfort and support.

We were driven there by my father. On arrival he went ahead and then came back, saying Aunty Bella did not want to see Ntombi, as any association with a black person would horrify the white residents. Ntombi waited in the car while I went up the narrow stairs to a little room stuffed with furniture. I had to look at the face of my father's sister through a red haze of rage.

When told she had died, I was indifferent. I was not interested when I learned that she had left us a cabinet from her room. We still have it in the lapa and call it Aunty Bella's cabinet. Whenever I notice that cupboard, I still seethe with anger, more than twenty years later.

Recently, while writing this chapter, I learned from Ntombi that she had been to Aunty Bella's funeral while I was at work. Ntombi would normally have been involved in the process, from washing the body to cooking and putting relatives up. Bella had been a devout Catholic, and Ntombi had lived and worshipped in a Catholic mission when in exile in Swaziland.

Ntombi and my father walked into a church hall to face an all-white congregation. Some people were openly hostile when they saw a black woman was attending the funeral. My father announced loudly that this was Ntombi, his daughter-in-law, and he held her hand the whole time they were there. We later visited members of the family who lived in Cape Town; they were warm and welcoming, as were other family members we got to know elsewhere.

Ntombi obtained a job with the company that was contracted to manage catering at the University of Cape Town. She was manager of one of the large kitchens attached to a student residence. Every night we would swap stories about our respective experiences. I would tell her about overhearing a black student shouting at a white professor: "You gave me the highest mark for an essay we both know is total crap. That is condescending and racist." She would tell me about catching a worker trying to steal a frozen chicken by stuffing it down the front of his trousers.

I was still completing my doctorate and was appointed as a junior lecturer in the Academic Development department with a tiny salary and an enormous workload. Seconded to Sociology, I had to teach classes of up to four hundred students while running a programme to support black students who were extremely bright but had huge gaps in their formal education. In addition, I had to assist other lecturers and participate in curriculum and materials development.

Ntombi took charge of improving our substantial house and small garden, squeezed onto a small plot in Rondebosch East, an area once set aside for coloured people. They faced intense racism from white working-class families who later moved into the area. A coloured woman lived with her grandson on one side of us. He worked for the same company as Ntombi, and the three of them often interacted.

A white divorced woman lived on the other side of us with five children, and every day their dogs shat on the neat lawn of the coloured woman. She showed Ntombi how she picked up the shit with newspaper and deposited it over the neighbour's gate. This was a skirmish in a larger war. I was sitting in our lounge when I overheard a man screaming racial abuse at someone, "You fokken rubbish, you hotnot, you mongrel."

Ntombi worked shifts at the kitchen, but she managed to organise her life so that, together with Gogo, she could run the home efficiently. Within days she got to know the street and neighbourhood, and the details of nearby families. Her main sources of intel were their domestic workers, her stop-and-chats, her sharp eyes, and her trips to the shops with our infant son Sipho tied to her back with his favourite blanket.

I was completely work centred, and it was one of the most difficult and richest environments I have known. The people I reported to and worked with were generally sharp, dedicated and supportive. We were all seized with the challenges facing the new South Africa. There were serious racial and political tensions, and the dominant culture of the university was suburban, English-speaking, white. Low salaries for junior staff served as a racial barrier that kept things exclusive. Black academics owed many kinds of debt and were not cushioned by well-off parents.

Within three years I had almost lost touch with my family and was beginning to burn out. Worse, I realised that I did not have the temperament to be an academic. By then I had been awarded a PhD by the University of Sunderland and suspected that my skills would be more in demand in places where I could make a larger contribution.

My first job application was accepted, and I informed Ntombi that I was to be a senior lecturer and deputy head of Academic Development at the University of Fort Hare in the Eastern Cape, at almost double the salary. It was increasingly difficult to survive on what I was earning at UCT, and the large jump to a senior lecturership was a significant career move.

For Ntombi, Gogo and our two children, it was the start of a great trek around South Africa as I was offered increasingly senior posts. Drunk on stress, I remained oblivious of the fact that I was part of a family and mostly ignored the impact of my decisions on others.

Fort Hare was a legendary site of anti-colonial struggle. For decades, it had been the only university open to black Africans, and the founding fathers of many southern African states had studied there before leading the fight for independence. The universities and townships of the Eastern Cape had been on the front line of the fight against apartheid, with the state deploying the military, death squads and systematic torture, among other repressive measures. The communities fought colonialism in the form of apartheid as it has always been fought, literally tooth and nail, and for every inch of physical, cultural and political space.

In Cape Town, I had been part of a team of mainly white academics, many being veterans of the struggle, who worked around the clock to transform teaching and the curriculum. We had to engage with an influx of extremely bright, angry and academically unprepared black students from the townships.

In Fort Hare, however, I found the university was parked alongside a sleepy town called Alice, which had a culture that must have driven the students mad. They were in a state of perpetual unrest, and with hindsight I sing their praises and hope our common political forebears are listening. Ntombi tells me that with sleepy ancestors, it is advisable to sneeze first to wake them up. This is why, I suppose, *sangomas* use a lot of snuff.

We had been told that though there was no property to rent or buy in Alice, the university could provide accommodation for new lecturers in the town. However, some senior staff stayed over in the houses during the week to avoid the ninety-minute drive to East London where many of them lived. It was rumoured that some used the accommodation to meet their lovers.

We were put up in a hotel on top of a mountain where eccentric people practising Buddhism, permaculture and veganism lived. Some of them were staff at the university. We made friends with a family, and they gave Busi a lift to the primary school in Alice that their daughter attended.

Every weekday I drove our little car down the mountain, dodging potholes and rocks, and then for twenty-five kilometres along a highway to Fort Hare. After six weeks I had yet to do one hour of serious work, and there was no prospect of finding suitable accommodation near the university. For a stress junky this was unbearable.

Although I was largely unaware of it, the bill for my job hopping was already high. We had sold a house that Ntombi and Gogo had lovingly developed in Cape Town. Our car was small and had no air conditioning. On the long trip up from Cape Town, toddler Sipho was sick and screamed incessantly for his Gogo and sister Busi, whom we had to leave in Cape Town with my parents. They followed by bus two weeks later, to live in damp hotel rooms. We had lost close friends and comrades. Busi and Sipho had been torn from their home, friends and family.

Ntombi and Gogo had to do the hard work of packing, moving and setting up a new home; and Ntombi's career had again been disrupted. And then, just as she was about to join a company set up to cater for Fort Hare, I decided we had to move again, and it was many painful months before she found work.

I applied for and obtained a post as a curriculum specialist in Mpumalanga, based at the provincial office in Middelburg, a sizeable town about two and a half hours' drive from Pretoria. The job, being in government, paid fifty per cent more than I was already earning, and was just within management echelons. My tolerant boss at Fort Hare was disappointed but understanding. He told me he had suspected that, like others, I would flee to work in the state.

Busi and Gogo took another bus back to Cape Town, twelve hours away, and with the intention of flying up to join us later. Ntombi packed our car to the roof, and we set off with Sipho down the long and perilous road to Mpumalanga. After a couple of weeks in a hotel, we rented half a semidetached house and drove to Johannesburg airport to pick up Busi and Sipho.

What we had not discussed, though it worried both of us, was that the apartheid Beast was largely hidden in Cape Town, and in retreat in the Eastern Cape, but still thrived on the large farms and small towns in provinces such as Mpumalanga.

A young Afrikaner family lived in the other half of the semidetached house we rented. The wife was beautiful in a wispy, delicate way, and smiled at us. Her son of about six was a silent child. Although there were no signs of physical abuse, it was clear that they were terrified of the husband, whose every movement was angry and violent.

I tried to suppress my fears for the woman and her child, not knowing how to intervene. Ntombi would have acted had we heard violence happening next door, but she would have relied on me to call the undoubtedly racist and sexist police. Gogo, who observed the family every day, saw them in purely human terms. "That devil man," she used to say, shaking her head.

Further down the road was a poor Afrikaner family, which included an elderly couple who came to visit often. Ntombi had been taught to be polite to the elderly from an early age, as indeed Afrikaner children are, and she always made them tea with biscuits. They out-talked Ntombi, whose sense of duty to the aged was stretched to the limit. She ended up trying to hide from them by putting her car in the garage so they would not know she was home. I was not aware of any of this, as I was already working long hours.

We bought a house with a large garden in a suburb of the town, assisted by an Afrikaner colleague with whom we had become close friends. Where we encountered the Beast was in the town centre, when Ntombi went to find a dentist. She was made to use the entrance and waiting room reserved for blacks and received rough treatment that damaged her teeth. She had a similar experience when she went to see a doctor. We had been back from exile for more than four years, but, because of my frequent uprooting, we had few political connections and were not sure what action to take. Five years later, I would have immediately contacted the Human Rights Commission and the media, and sued for the injury to Ntombi's dignity and teeth.

We did consult the ANC mayor, a good man we knew from exile, and suggested that we work with ANC branches in the township to mount a campaign. From his response, we gathered that dealing with racist doctors would not be a priority for them, considering the injustices that they encountered every day.

In 1997, having bought a more comfortable car, we made the long trip to Cape Town to visit my family. Staying in a guest house in Colesberg, halfway there, we attracted stares, and I worried about the car. We left early the next day. A friendly and puzzled white couple who had parked next to us had their tyres slashed. We did not stop to explain what had happened, something that still niggles at my conscience.

It was another year before Ntombi and I worked up the courage to leave the children with Gogo in our suburban house and spend a weekend in a nearby holiday resort. We chose Bela-Bela, the new name for the hot springs that used to be called Warmbaths. Such renaming generated a lot of tension in the Afrikaner community, which is why we used the old name when asking the way. Fearing the prices in restaurants, we decided to shop for provisions in a rural general store, which was crowded with goods and people as is usual on a Saturday morning.

Two gangly Afrikaner youths were acting aggressively, rolling their eyes at us, and lurching about. In the queue one got behind us, and I clutched at the knife I kept in my pocket. I turned to look at him and he gave us a huge grin, saying, "'Scuse us, uncle, we got Bela-Bela babalas." They were in the grip of a violent hangover.

When I told this story to my English brother-in-law, he confessed that he had thought "babalas" was the local name for haemorrhoids. We explained it was a beloved South African word, probably derived from a isiZulu word for being drunk.

I was to move jobs and houses three times more before we settled down near Pretoria. Ntombi became an army officer and I moved to the Department of Home Affairs after thirty years in education. The department is responsible for citizenship, identity and immigration, and I headed strategic planning, policy and monitoring. This lateral move revived my energies, and I urge all middle-aged people to do likewise – be it ballet or quantum mechanics – if they have only known one kind of work.

I kept generating stress, but at least I stopped moving around. Before we retired and with the children still at home, Ntombi declared our house near Pretoria to be the family home. She had finally grown roots since returning after decades in exile, and she vowed her children would always have this home to return to and inherit. That is one commitment I will respect. Ntombi states very forcefully that she is worn out by my abusing her over decades and that her joints shriek when she moves.

Twelve

It changed us forever

Awake at night –
the sound of the water jar
cracking in the cold
– Matsuo Basho, Japanese poet (1644–94)

ON 23 MARCH 2020, President Cyril Ramaphosa addressed the nation and announced the level five lockdown would last for twenty-one days, starting at midnight after three days. The lockdown was later extended by a week or so. I joined the throngs buying enough supplies to survive Armageddon, ignoring sensible government advice that essential goods would be available. Somehow, I managed to get technicians in to ensure our solar water and electrical systems were in good order. They had cost me a big chunk of my savings, but I read the signs and realised our ship of state was sinking fast.

Everyone except certain categories of people would have to stay in their houses unless they had to shop for food, be paid out a grant or seek medical attention. The army would help the police to carry out strict enforcement that was humane and helpful. I wished the president a lot of luck with that last point. No real soldier will stop your car and read a letter explaining why only you could find a folder in your manager's hard drive.

It occurred to me that since Nomvula left childhood behind and moved to her husband's clan she has always been locked down. First it was as a young *makoti*, tied to her husband's family in a rural settlement. She uses the word "slave" to describe her role. Then came another form of lockdown, in the servant's room of a white family in apartheid South Africa, looking after other people's children.

And, finally, Nomvula came to live with us so our children would enjoy the company of their Gogo, after we returned from exile. We were hundreds of kilometres away in suburbs that were still largely white after a quarter-century of the new South Africa. An enforced lockdown put us all in her element, and she responded by becoming more confident and assertive.

That change was the first of many subtle transformations brought about by Covid-19. It also brought our daughter Busi back to us, at least until the end of level five, as she had parted with her partner of five years on the eve of lockdown and would be working from home. She was already under emotional stress, but we looked forward to having her with us. Our son and his partner Tiaan occupied a townhouse we owned in a complex nearby, but neither of them had permission to leave their home, so we would not be seeing them.

Ntombi's life is regulated by her medication for severe arthritis of the joints and her crumbling bones. Most days she is asleep by one in the morning and wakes around ten to sit at the dining room table and hold court. She enjoys having me around and I am careful not to be absent too often. One morning at breakfast I wrote down a typical Covid-19 conversation.

Ntombi said, "This Minister of Health is taking charge. He even respects traditional medicine."

I said that in fighting this virus, of course they should involve *izinyanga* like her uncle Abel and spiritual healers like *sangomas* too. Over sixty per cent of mainly black South Africans go to them, rich and poor, and they have white clients as well.

"Even ministers," Ntombi pointed out. She half rose from her chair and transitioned into her acting mode. She seemed to expand, and her voice was deeper and louder. "You with your modern ways have no force because you cannot call on your ancestors. You are retired but if your former Director-General called you now, it would be 'Yes DG, of course DG. I will write the ten pages for you right now.'" For a minute Ntombi became me and answered the DG in a pathetic, whining voice. "And you will sit and do it instead of telling him it is your family time. If it was me, the ancestors will speak through my mouth and it will come out like a lion!" Ntombi gave a huge roar, frightening me.

I suggested that I could call up my dead father or, even better, my mother. She was dismissive.

"You don't know how. You never burned the right plants to make that incense. And there are other ceremonies. We always keep goats so we can call our ancestors. When you kill a goat, it cries to them very loudly, and that is why we use goats and not sheep: to wake them up."

In the morning Ntombi efficiently stalks around on her artificial knees and does routine cleaning and washing, leaving time to expertly and creatively cook and garden. Evenings are for watching TV with Gogo and then sitting up in bed and working her phone with one eye on news channels and reality shows. She networks and researches topics that may be political, social, medical or environmental. I sometimes smell fake news and complain, if I feel bold or angry enough. I am told to keep quiet one minute, and the next minute am engaged in conversation, and heaven help me if I am not paying attention.

My personal response to the lockdown is to avoid emotional stress by creating or reviving multiple projects that keep me busy. This is typical of a workaholic. Ntombi is deeply suspicious of some types of projects, as my workaholism has caused her mental and physical anguish over many years. If I do not cut my ties with Home Affairs soon, she warns me, you will find all your computers smashed and in the dustbin. Ntombi was referring to a contract I was grappling with, to draft a national policy on one-stop border posts.

We have a lapa, which Ntombi improved after we bought the house. It is a brick-and-canvas structure by the pool filled with a large table that is meant for entertainment but is not much used, except when I have a meeting or use it as a temporary office. After breakfast on the fifteenth day of the lockdown, I went to the lapa to work and yawn every two minutes. I soon went indoors to count my Nespresso capsules and make a cup of coffee.

I found Ntombi busy in the kitchen. She handed me a bowl of the pulp of granadillas, straight off the vine, mixed with double cream yoghurt and some sweet grapes she had found in the fridge. We are running short of fresh fruit and nothing else in the garden is ripe. The tart taste of the granadilla and the crunchy seeds perfectly offset the smooth yogurt and sweet juicy grapes. I love my wife and her food, although she agrees with the American actress Roseanne Barr, who says, "The quickest way to a man's heart is through his chest."

I began to spend more time in the garden than I had ever done. Our winter weather is glorious, with crispy nights and clear warm days. In the first weeks of the lockdown, it was still warm enough for me to heat up a bowl of oats for breakfast and eat it in the garden. Once, I looked up and saw that the "inverted bowl of the sky", as Omar Khayyam puts it, was an astonishing deep blue. The last time the sky was that colour was probably when my mother was a child, before the area around Johannesburg became the industrial heartland of the country. Now the heart had stopped beating for four weeks because of the virus, and the colour of the sky had changed. Ntombi commented that this should tell us all to change our modern ways.

Thinking about what Ntombi had said, I wished we were transported back to the 1920s and then realised there might be drawbacks. Back then, there had been a law forbidding black persons to walk on the pavements. Ntombi would have complained every time her platinum implants were jolted when she stepped in muddy potholes. Also, my fuzzy little mother several times told me how, as a Jew, she was often chased down the same pavements by children hurling rocks and screaming "Christ killer". I would have had to carry a heavy cane in case I wanted to correct the little Christians and ensure their spiritual well-being.

I walked down the garden, past Busi's bedroom, on my way to wash my bowl in the kitchen. She was already in a video conference. "Is there any way you can switch off the birds?" she asked me through the window. "They are so loud that the team thinks I am sitting in the garden."

Ntombi was cleaning the small yard behind our kitchen, which was formed by the back of our garden flat and shoulder-high walls. She had it roofed over with corrugated plastic sheets and built a storeroom in one corner. The same type of canvas we had used in the lapa closes the gap between the wall, and it was unzipped and rolled up.

Our clothes are dried in the yard and there is a spare gas stove for cooking things like jam and steamed bread, plus an old Whirlpool washing machine for heavy washes. Ntombi loves that machine and keeps it alive. My hope and belief is that I will receive the same standard of care as my parts wear out. She made and fitted the replacement tubing and washers herself. The yard had shelves on which we stored bulk goods, from soap powder to toilet paper. Among the supplies I had bought were sacks of beans and samp, similar to the maize kernels Americans call grits.

"I found rats," she reported, sweeping up the samp and other food that had escaped from holes made by the rodents. "Some have eaten the poison cakes I put out and will die, but others did not." She began sweeping away the scraps of toilet paper the rats were building nests with. "I will show you a YouTube of how to make a trap from this." She handed me a five-litre transparent bottle that had once held vinegar.

I was thrilled. Not only was I being trusted with a practical task, but, like any husband, I love fiddling with gadgets. It also suggested that Ntombi thought I was smarter than a rat. She has a high regard for them as clever and industrious creatures and lectured me on their ways over lunch. With the tiniest change of facial expression and movements of her head and shoulders, she became a rat. One of her most amazing talents is the ability to transform herself into any familiar animal, including humans. I expected her to sprout whiskers.

After more than a month of a level five lockdown, the President announced we would move to a more relaxed level four. Among the new measures, we would be able to walk around our neighbourhood for three hours per day, between six and nine in the morning.

My daily constitutional became the most regular of my routines, surpassing my t'ai chi warm-ups and drills. Two weeks into May, winter arrived. I left the house early for my walk while everyone else was asleep. Breath escapes my mask and fogs up the inside of my spectacles. The rays of the rising sun light up the fog, so I am walking in a bright haze. I return greetings while not knowing if the dog pulling my neighbours along is a chihuahua or a rottweiler. It becomes a little warmer as the sun rises and most of the fog vanishes.

The next day I was passed by two elderly joggers. They were unmasked, illegal, and looked happy. I remembered a catchy song and whispered an adaptation to myself.

I'm a jogger
I'm a blogger
an old-age snogger
And you have got me on the run

Behind my mask I could be sad, bad or glad, and they would never know.

I was addicted to the Netflix series *Bordertown*, a psychological detective thriller set in Finland. The town was filled with psychopaths, depressed detectives, and angst, alienation and anomie. I wondered if the *Bordertown* series was attracting or repelling tourists to Finland.

My watching of the episode was interrupted. Ntombi and Gogo were sitting in our bedroom, and I heard a terrible row. I hurried from one end of the house to the other to check on them and found them sharing a home-grown story in isiZulu and laughing loudly.

"Is everything OK?" was my way of saying, "Please tell me what it is about."

Ntombi replied. "You know my uncle Abel likes me – no, loves me – because I tell the truth."

Animated, Ntombi repeated the story Abel had told them about one of his relatives, which was biting and funny and sad – how people lied to themselves and others to protect their dreams, which were worthless. Abel had lent the man money to buy petrol so he could go to a funeral in a borrowed car. This made a good first impression when he arrived at the funeral, but he had no way of bringing food or drink to contribute, as was the custom.

"All he could do was open his mouth and hope for food, but the only visitor to his mouth was the flies, as we say in Zulu."

Rowdy laughter came from Ntombi and Gogo.

Ntombi is indeed the Truth Teller, the one who holds a mirror to people. Those who can learn from her will one day love her. Others might hate her, but she is fearless.

I have seen her go to great lengths after discovering wrong was being done to a family member. She even allied with her estranged father to get one of his children to do the right thing and marry a woman he had lived with and relied on for years.

Recently a friend of ours died, and a grandchild who stayed with her was left behind. The child was cared for by her granny after the violent death of her mother. Ntombi believed the girl child and her inheritance were in grave danger of being taken advantage of by scheming relatives and dubious social workers. Ntombi, with no legal training, successfully defended the child in and out of court, and ensured she was united with the father, who stayed with his loving family in a rural area.

The lockdown has helped me get to the roots of Ntombi by observing more closely how she sees everything in family terms. Her world view, her morality and her decisions are governed by this.

One day she showed me a family of dead rats. "The mother ate the poison I put out and died. See how her babies starved." There was sympathy and understanding in Ntombi's voice but absolutely no regret. The rats were attacking our food stockpile and had to go. In the same way, a director-general told me that you must never fire any employee in anger. Kill like a lion because a lion does not hate its prey.

If Ntombi sees me throwing a branch with undeveloped granadillas on the compost heap, she will know which of the many vines it comes from and will tell me that they are undeveloped because that spot lacks sun or the soil is deficient. She will explain how one purple fruit is almost developed enough to pick, because its position on the vine allows it more food than the others. But it failed to make it in time and now had to rot in the compost heap for the future good of its brothers and sisters.

This is Ntombi's proudly peasant notion of tough love.

Thinking about this, I recalled that when Ntombi remembers a disaster of my making, her face sometimes crumbles and becomes wet with tears. My insides churn and I want to smash my head against a wall. We had decided to build a flat on top of our garage and extending over a carport. I hired a crooked builder who presented the lowest bid, and I then failed to supervise the work. I was under pressure from my own job, was soft and indecisive, and I knew little about the details of building. Ntombi is the opposite on all three counts but had to go into hospital for a double knee replacement. Chaos ensued that resulted in years of stress, pain and expense. Ntombi had built the house we live in for the children, and I had betrayed the family.

I asked Ntombi what she thought winter would be like, short or long.

"It will be a short, hard winter."

"How do you know?"

"I feel it. When we moved here, winter would start as early as February or March. Now it can be May or June."

"That is probably climate change, but will it confuse the *mchicha*?" I used the Kiswahili word for African spinach that we had learned in Tanzania.

I asked this because Ntombi knows more about the habits of African spinach than any other plant; and it is the food Africans have always depended on. Sometime Ntombi stops the car and harvests *mchicha* growing by the side of the road if it is producing seeds.

"Of course. It is supposed to come in spring. From the seeds that fall in summer. It could grow as early as November."

I turned to ask Ntombi's mother, who was going to be eighty-four soon.

"Gogo, Ntombi's bones tell her it will be a short winter. What do your old bones tell you?""

"It will be long."

"So, whose bones are telling me the truth? Your *amathambo* or Ntombi's?"

"My bones."

"Whatever your bones tell you, Gogo, it is cold in your room, we must get you a husband or an electric blanket. Where can I find a husband and perhaps pick up a cow or two in lobola?"

"Abel – he gave us food when Ntombi was small."

Being largely ignorant about such matters, I did not know whether Gogo meant that Abel would marry her, or whether he would supply the lobola. What I knew is that Gogo is a valued member of my family. She maintains the peace, enriches our lives, keeps Ntombi sane (although she often tells her, in isiZulu, she is mad) and irons for an average of perhaps sixty minutes a day. As I understand it, the main purpose of lobola is to unite the two families and clans, and to compensate the bride's family for lost labour. I would want plenty of lobola for Gogo.

That night, Ntombi put an electric blanket in Gogo's bed, cursing me for interfering because the last time she tried that, Gogo became too hot and threw off the bedclothes.

For a long while, because of retirement, Ntombi and I had been keeping crazy hours. Now it was made worse by the lockdown, which among other things has killed the seven-day week. We often ask each other what day it is. Every few days Ntombi takes heavy meds and sleeps until the late afternoon. She then is bright and breezy, chattering through dinner and into the evening. At that time, I am winding down, as I get up around six or earlier, after going to bed at one. I sometimes have power naps before breakfast or after lunch if I am working on something intense.

We have a problem in that that we are loud, especially me, being thoughtless and deaf, as Ntombi points out. We are not used to having Busi back in the house and she is amazingly quiet, shut up in her two-and-a-half-by-three-metre room with a tiny desk I fitted into a nook. She uses earphones with a mike and keeps her voice down, moving between the desk and her bed depending on the nature of the call or video conference and the shifting boundaries between her working and social lives.

Busi began to keep this up for twelve hours straight, only sneaking out to grab some food or take a shower. She did ask me to help her with a radio voice-over she was doing for a friend, which she will be paid for if he sells the advert. It was a Sunday. Meet the new working class, made out of a salad of contracts, a spoonful of self-employed petit bourgeois, and a soupçon of the lumpenproletariat, who live by their wits.

At about ten pm she came into our bedroom to ask for an eye mask. She had dropped hers and could not find it, her room being waist-high with clothes, equipment, bags, toiletries and other stuff. Two hours later, as midnight approached, she knocked and entered. She was in her jimjams and gown, and an eye mask was on top of her head.

"Let me tell you, you people are loud as fuck."

We looked accusingly at each other.

"You are both loud as fuck. The way you talk, the way you walk around at all hours. Just put on the alarm and go to sleep. He is deaf, you want to argue. What it comes down to is that you are loud as fuck."

We looked down, ashamed of ourselves, and she went back to bed.

***

As we settled into our stage four lockdown, I noticed the cloudscapes that arch over our house. A cargo plane from the nearby air force base lumbered across the horizon, a shade darker than the rain clouds building up. Flocks of swallows darted in formation with shrill cries that carried for a kilometre or more.

Then I saw three hadadas sitting on the ridge of the neighbours' double-storeyed house, hunched in their glossy coats like a trio of lawyers, curved beaks opening to emit harsh cries. As a white child I was taught about the mythology of ancient Greece and Rome and not that of Africa. Ancient Egypt was not considered part of Africa, and I remembered that the bird we call a hadada is related to the sacred ibis, associated in ancient Egypt with Thoth, the god of wisdom, art, judgement and the dead. I looked at the birds and saw that their presence did not augur well.

I decided to keep this information to myself and went indoors as the first drops of rain made spreading circles on the surface of the swimming pool. It was day eight of the Covid-19 lockdown. It was a soft soothing rain that drizzled down for the next two days and it reminded me of a song that minstrels tramping about in the sixteenth century used to sing:

> Westron wynde, when wilt thou blow,
> The small raine down can raine.
> Cryst, if my love were in my armes
> And I in my bedde again

Those words, with modern spelling, are on a framed picture above my bed. I asked my sister Ruth, who is a wonderful artist, to illustrate the song for my sixtieth birthday present. In the picture the words are flying around with lovers and wind-blown trees, rather like brides and cows in a Chagall painting, except that Ruth works with oil pastels. In my locked-down state, instead of love, the picture reminds me to relish my comfort and look down on damp minstrels singing for their suppers. This was another of the Covid-19 transformations.

Several of the people I phoned to chat with told me that things were hectic despite their being at home, because the crisis had doubled their businesses. One was in logistics, two were in financial services, and several in IT. I told them it was all about the 4IR and began analysing socio-economic trends for them. They told me politely to get the hell off the phone as they were rather busy.

Ntombi was still plugged into her social networks and shared a stream of Covid-19 news with me. This included the pandemic's impact on friends and family, what the disease can do to the lungs, and the efforts being made by the defence force. She would catch me in the corridor or bathroom and share her own analysis with me, based on things she had noted or conversations she was having.

People were starting to think and feel differently, and their values were changing. The grip that consumerism had on them was loosened and they vowed to live cleaner lives and value human beings and nature above things. When she called Ruth, my sister had said, "It's like nature just phoned us and told us to watch out, we better learn to live simpler, better lives."

Ntombi told me that she agreed one hundred per cent with Ruth.

I shouted, "You are both right," over my shoulder as I scurried about. I had not grasped the importance of her thoughts because I was seized with pessimism.

I often told Ntombi that even if we lived simply, we would still starve in South Africa. We had been downgraded to junk status, the rand and the economy would collapse, and our leaders had no viable solution because they depended on what Ntombi calls "leeching off the state". My investments and government pension were worth perhaps twenty per cent less in real terms than a week earlier.

Frightening myself, I would go and water the herbs, tomatoes and a lime tree I had planted in the pots I bought just before the lockdown. The lime tree was months away from bearing fruit, and that was a good thing. It would not tempt me to consider a gin and tonic. Busi and I enjoy a tipple, and I had a bottle hidden somewhere, but it did not seem right or safe to booze during a deadly pandemic.

One night I was restless, plagued not by the virus but by Ruth's and Ntombi's thoughts. They had the ring and sting of truth. Earlier that evening I had forwarded to several people an article by Arundhati Roy that explores such ideas: "The pandemic is a portal". The novelist was smelling the same sea change that I was.

My own research suggested that humanity was on the cusp of a shift in consciousness, and we will be nudged over the edge by the virus and the 4IR. It will achieve something like what the bubonic plague had done when it killed off thirty per cent of European peasants, forcing feudal lords to offer wages, and unleashing the capitalist system and a new world view.

But what is being unleashed? Perhaps it is W.B. Yeats's foul beast, slouching towards Bethlehem to be born. I would rather believe in the prophetic power of Hollywood, Netflix, Showmax and the purveyors of video games. They seem to suggest that the new world will have an elite that live with armed robots in domed cities, here or off-world, while the rest of us roam across wastelands, gasping for oxygen and fighting for human flesh.

Or perhaps we will escape that fate and have a digital democracy, powered by well-governed and ethical capitalism, where all can realise their dreams. You, gentle reader, can weigh things up and decide.

I decided that I was going to seek the answer in ancient Chinese poetry. Perhaps we were experiencing the kind of shift in consciousness that gave rise, at about the same time, to the humanistic teachings of Socrates, Confucius and the Buddha, according to a Netflix documentary.

I was not lockdown crazy, the equivalent of being *bosbefokked* (bush-fucked), an apartheid-era term for a maddened white soldier who starts screaming and sprays the bushes with bullets. My inspiration came from mysterious symbols that appeared on the bubble blanket I use to cover my swimming pool so as to conserve water and thus save money and the planet. It floats on top and prevents the water from evaporating. Rows of white signs started appearing on the dark blue plastic.

I photographed them, and an image search suggested they resembled early Chinese ideographs. The rational part of my brain reminded me that I put salt in my pool to be converted by a chlorinator. The glyphs were made by the water getting on the plastic cover and drying, leaving behind salt patterns. "Ah," a *sangoma* might say, "but why did it dry in those patterns? Are your ancestors not calling to you?"

Reading ancient Chinese poetry seemed the right thing to do. I downloaded the best collection I could find onto my Kindle, even though half my money had evaporated and the value of the rand had dropped like a rock. The curator and translator, David Hinton, explained in his book that the earliest poems are a fusion of popular oral poetry, Chinese ideographs, a literary form of Chinese, and a world view which underwent a profound shift towards humanism.

Excited by this analysis, I began searching for a poem, the one that would signify a changing world view. The first stage of thousands of years of written poetry produced praises of state religion by theocrats. Next, there was a time of total war and disintegration, with Taoist poems on good governance and the value of being human. Finally, I saw a poem that was intensely personal and somehow infused with love. I found a typical verse that I liked, "Seventh Moon" from the great *Book of Songs*, said to be compiled by Confucius.

Seventh moon, Fire Star ebbs away,
And ninth, we share out warm robes.

By the tenth moon, chill winds howl
And by the eleventh it's bitter cold

And indeed, because it is autumn and the sun's warmth is ebbing away, Ntombi appeared after supper with our winter bedclothes in her arms. She called me to perform our annual ritual, which involves me helping her to replace our bed cover and blanket with a padded duvet and warm sheet. Ntombi gave me the usual sermon about how pathetic it is for a grown man not to know how to put a cover on a duvet.

I crept back to bed, snuggled under the duvet and I fell into a deep sleep, only to be woken by Ntombi cleaning the room. She had started her autumn cleaning routine and it would continue for days. What was not normal was that it was two in the morning. I sensed that her behaviour was related to lockdown. I was woken again by Ntombi at six and instructed to go check on Gogo and clean the corridor and bathrooms. The voice of Empress Ntombi was imperious, and I complied. She eventually returned to bed and fell asleep. Her snores are soothing and listening to them I soon nodded off.

The silence we hear during stages five and four of lockdown is music to the ears of genuine insomniacs. In the small hours all you can hear is the blood in your ears, singing softly of the sea. You start seeing screen savers that your retina generates in its resting state. What keeps you awake, however, are the stray thoughts that gnaw away like rats. Out of boredom you seize one and begin dissecting it, trying not to remember the look on the face of the rat you had to dissect in high school. Our street is quiet at that time, and I thought about silence and how powerful it can be in a conversation, a poem or a film.

I thought about the film that changed my world view the most: *The Tree of Wooden Clogs*, directed by Ermanno Olmi, which is set in Italy in the 1900s. A farm worker cut a tree down to make clogs for his daughter so she could go to school. The family was quietly expelled from the farm. The final scene lasted about five seconds, showing them in a cellar, somewhere, staring into the darkness and quietly starving.

***

I hardly ever share stories of my childhood with Ntombi. In exploring my past, I am largely limited to my often suppressed memory and the collective family record, some of which I could access during the lockdown by contacting people online or searching the internet. My memories are often blocked by past trauma and strong emotions, especially at a subconscious level. Instead of trying to recall my past systematically, I must wade through a soup made of what artefacts remain and other people's memories, looking for scraps of my history.

Ntombi views the past far more coherently as she has two advantages. Firstly, she had an amazingly detailed and accurate memory, although her very early childhood is hazy. Secondly, her belief in her traditions allows her to access a traditional knowledge system and people that are organised on many levels, social, spiritual, psychological and linguistic.

Her spiritual system is supported by a rational and observant mind informed by her years in exile in many countries. Unlike mine, her views are pragmatic and generally free of the abstractions of formal social science or institutionalised religions. These give me a viewpoint that is largely disconnected from individuals and families, which are the elements that largely populate Ntombi's world view.

Despite our different perspectives and cultures, most of the time we communicate quite effectively and find common ground. This is so in part because we were formed by similar experiences and a shared historical context, and also because over thirty years our thoughts and feelings began to merge.

In the first months of the lockdown, Ntombi switched to story-telling mode, starting with her early years. Her voice changed, her eyes widened, and she became physically animated, even when seated. Living with us, Busi also benefited from hearing the stories. She and Sipho had yet to visit Kwamteyi, although they had visited Ntombi's family in Ladysmith and Swaziland. As Ntombi spoke, Gogo looked interested; she smiled and drank tea. I kept quiet. I was thinking that sixty-four years ago Gogo looked after the infant Ntombi so that she could be sitting beside me, telling me this story.

As Ntombi grew up, she always joined in the culture of the people she was living with, and was known for her dancing and singing. Until her arthritis and crumbling joints prevented her, she would suddenly do spectacular dance moves that she learned when a young exile in Zambia, West Africa and Cuba. Sadly, she will usually sing only at funerals – and I am sure my funeral – or when she sings "Happy birthday". She lifts her head and suddenly this clear, soaring voice fills the room.

One of Ntombi's earliest memories is of a bent-nosed woman called Margaret, who took the toddler to Zionist church meetings. The way was long, and thorns pricked Ntombi's unshod feet. Now and again, Margaret picked up the child to comfort her. What Ntombi remembers of the Zionist meetings is the loud drums and singing. Ntombi's family on both sides were affiliated to churches brought by missionaries, and her mother's family had built several churches and congregations.

Ntombi spent most of her teens in a Catholic mission in Swaziland and sang in the choir, but she had always taken Zulu traditions more seriously. She learned to dance from an early age. I reminded Ntombi that we had received a wedding DVD from relatives in Swaziland, with the two clans dancing in matching traditional dress. I was impressed, but Ntombi snorted like a she-buffalo.

"You see the girls with their bush knives – that is not dancing. You must show how you defend your honour, your family and your clan. Any boy who came near me found out quick. At the Reed Dance that the Swazi King calls every year to celebrate, he may even choose a bride. I jumped in the air and showed how I would use the knife. Once my father had to tell people to pull me away as the King might choose me, the way I was dancing."

Sitting at dinner, Ntombi asked her mother to look for a green photo album in her cupboard. My wife opened the album, which she had put together before she met me. In it was a studio photo of Ntombi before the Reed Dance, where thousands of Swazi virgins present reeds to the King. The bare-breasted Ntombi was holding a machete at the ready and was staring down the camera with steely eyes.

"You know, before we left home, where I was a child, Gogo would get up very early. She made fire and prepared sour porridge for the family and hot water for tea. People passing by would ask, 'Have you got stiff porridge?' They would eat pieces of left-over porridge with tea, then thank her and go on their way."

"Did they pay?" I asked.

"Never, there was real *ubuntu* those days. My family never thanked Gogo, and she did so much for them." Gogo smiled and shook her head sadly.

I sometimes use the word "pirates" to refer to the people who looted our ship of state before and during the saga known as state capture and are still grabbing what they can. Far more South Africans use the word to refer to one of the two most popular football clubs, Pirates and Chiefs. At dinner, I introduced the topic by asking Ntombi which team she preferred. Normally, we never discuss football beyond making comments when watching a televised international match.

Ntombi became excited and asked me why I wanted to know. I thought of stories about husbands and wives divorcing because they belong to the rival football clubs, but that would surely not apply to us. When I mentioned it had to do with my writing project, she said that football is important in her culture.

"As children we loved the Pirates, because to us the skeletons on the flags mean dead people and dead people come alive in the spirit world, especially at night. How can you lose with the spirits behind you? Especially now the teams play at night. It is like we mix our culture with the game.

"At night we would run past the place where you dip the cattle. It is by a little river that is dried now. There were thousands of lights and we did not know they are made by flying worms. People would tell us: 'See, this is their time. The spirits are coming, they are moving.'" Ntombi took a sip of tea.

"We children liked the idea of the spirits fighting the Amakhosi, the Chiefs. If the Chiefs won, it was also okay – they are royalty after all, with their kings. It was a big thing also in Swaziland. Every family could be seen putting the batteries of their little radios in the sun to get them working. Batteries were hard to get."

Ntombi continued: "My father said it was important to support where you come from, so his team was AmaZulu. When they played, everyone crowded around those radios. And children kept very still. If a child spoke, someone could even whip with a stick and knock them down!" She half rose from her seat and whipped her arm across the table, missing me by a millimetre.

"There was a community spirit around sports. The same when a play came on at seven o'clock like about King Shaka. It was very important. Those announcers and readers, they deserve to have an award. Their voice and the way they describe things. We had nothing in those days. They were bringing something that you could see that it's alive, yet it was on the radio. Watching TV is a dead thing."

Ntombi looked thoughtful. "That spirit – it should be there when we discuss what will happen with the land. I want a farm; farming is part of me. The land must come to us, but instead of fighting over the land, we must work together and focus on producing. We are talking about it the wrong way."

I asked Ntombi if I should put the same question to Gogo, about which team she supported, Pirates or Chiefs.

"She is not interested in football. In her generation women were never involved. It was my generation where women sat around, listening to games being discussed. But she did men's things in the house, as her brothers were away working in Johannesburg."

One evening, Ntombi had been on her phone for a long time while I was reading. "I have just been communicating with Roy on the phone," she told me. "I stayed with his family when I was a child and he was like a brother. I remember how he used to win fights with his bull. The boys even made up praise poems that they sang to their beasts."

Ntombi tossed her head, just like a bull, and was claimed by her memories again. "He would whistle that slogan only his bull knew, and the bull would respond." Ntombi whistled softly, and I asked if the bulls got killed.

"No, one always walks away. Like you chased away that man who wanted me when you and I started going together. And the calves and cows get out of the way. When a beast was slaughtered the herdboys always got the lungs to roast, up on the mountain. But Roy loved his bull, he would go up to the kraal at night with a broken bottle and sharpen those long horns. 'You will see how he fights tomorrow,' Roy would tell us.

"If a herdboy could not find one of the animals, he did not dare come home until he found it. The mother would leave some food out where we cook. He would creep in, very quiet and shivering. He would find a corner to lie down and be out when it was light, to continue looking."

On another occasion, we watched on the news as a young opposition MP tormented the Deputy President, an old bull who had made a speech about the fourth industrial revolution. "And what exactly is nanotechnology?" asked the grinning young MP at question time. He had grown up in a village and in townships but was also plugged into new knowledge systems. The Deputy President tried to hide his ignorance but failed.

The word "technology" pulled some more memories out of Ntombi. "We had no electricity in those days. We used to walk half a day to take our mielie harvest to be ground. Everyone had a bag on their head and others were piled high on the back of a donkey. Our power came from donkeys and cattle. We saw they could carry and pull things, and used them. That was how our industrial revolution began."

I reminded Ntombi that, when we lived in Tanzania, the government used slogans to encourage animal power, like "donkeynisation" and "oxenisation", but she would not be distracted. This time she asked Busi to retrieve the green photo album.

Ntombi failed to find a photo of Nobango, her paternal grandmother, whose popular name was Beauty. She was tall and had huge hips, just one of them big enough to make a child out of. Ntombi tells us how Beauty "infected" all the girls in her line with huge hips, good for making children, some of them from too many fathers. Without getting off her seat, by quick movements and a change of voice, Ntombi became her grandmother talking to her children. Busi and I crowded round the book as Ntombi told us about the people in each photograph.

Gogo left the table to do the washing-up. When I tried to insist that I would do it, Gogo told me I was naughty and she would beat me. Sometimes she added that she would stick a big needle in me. Normally her tone was light, but this time she was serious. I was trespassing on her territory.

"You don't know that Gogo is clever? I worked many years for that white family. Shopping, and looking after children and the sick wife. Picking her up on the bed. I come from a village, but I don't take nonsense.

"I told my husband, Shoti, stop playing with nurses or I will kill you. And I did the same for that wife of Abel. She would put Vicks in her eyes to make them red, tell us she was sick, and so I had to fetch water, all the wood. Then she told me to do all of her work or she would kill me. I told her I have a chopper and a long bush knife. She smiled and never touched me. You are naughty – sit down."

It was the longest speech I had ever heard Gogo make in English.

Thirteen

Stress tests and biting intestines

When you realise how perfect everything is, you will tilt your head back and laugh at the sky.
– The Buddha

ONE MORNING SOME clockwork in my subconscious woke me up at exactly three thirty, again. It ignored Ntombi's pleas and warnings not to disturb her healing sleep. Every itch-prone bit of me began to itch, and I knew why. It wanted me to be seated in front of a keyboard in the corner of the bedroom where Ntombi had built me an office. I began to regret doing a deal with my subconscious the day before. The senior official at Home Affairs managing my contract had called me and said, "The document is ready to go to the minister. Except that it needs a better first paragraph."

My heart shrivelled to the size of a peanut. My books had been exiled by Ntombi to my dusty library along a wall of the garage. Amongst them is *Strange Pilgrims*, a book of stories written shortly before his death by the master, Gabriel García Márquez. His preface contains advice to writers, and the direst warning was about first paragraphs.

Marquez wrote that if the opening works, writing the rest of the manuscript will be the closest a human can get to flying. If it does not, give up the project: or if you fail, you will experience the torments of hell, and even suffer physical harm.

After rewriting the paragraph, I returned to the land of Nod and slept like the baby Jesus until seven. I had interesting, stress-free dreams that I remembered after waking. Ntombi woke up and switched on her phone, causing me to freeze. Then she went back to sleep. The phone lit up the subtle planes of her face and an angelic smile.

The Home Affairs guy later confirmed that the paragraph was much better and that the job was done. I quickly wrapped up and submitted my close-up report. A few weeks later they signed my last invoice. I informed a wary Ntombi that I would never again work on contract for them and managed to get a guarded kiss and a hug.

Due to the post-retirement contract job I had not cooked for a long while. Then the pressure eased off and I announced I would do some cooking. In the kitchen I reached up and got down the wok I lovingly kept black and smooth, much as my wife Ntombi pampers her skin with lotions improved with herbs from the garden. Something distracted me and I forgot about preparing the meal.

The next day Ntombi reminded me of my promise, which was unusual. This was one of the many subtle changes in our household after our respective retirements. Usually, she would allow my sins of omission to pile up and use them tactically as ammunition against me. I replied that in one hour the stir fry would be ready and told the ladies that we must be seated by then and ready to eat.

Bang on time, Gogo collected her bowl and spoon, and we sat down. The chunky vegetables were just crunchy enough. Ntombi was faffing around in the kitchen complaining about Mr Untidy, who had left the kitchen in a filthy state. I complained bitterly in turn about a wife who sabotaged his every attempt at cooking. By the time she sat down I was steaming, and the food was cold.

Ntombi smiled, joining us at the table, and began doing something with her fork and a napkin. "See, when I buy a fork, I bend it under a cloth in the shop. This is a strong fork." I was angry and over-acted the part of an abused spouse. "You subject it to a stress test. Like you do your husband. But me, you stress-test every day. The fork thing you do just the once."

One source of stress and admiration is the high standards Ntombi sets for sustainability and frugal living. Ntombi handed me her bowl to take to the kitchen one morning after breakfast. "Put this in your book." In the clean bowl, I saw a shining spoon and a small ball of damp paper containing traces of porridge and milk. "I used one tablespoon of water," she told me. "Just rinse it and put it to dry. The paper goes in the bucket for the compost heap. The compost needs a bit of water. We are a nation of extravagance. That is how we did it when we lived without taps."

The radio was tuned to SAfm. It told Ntombi that somewhere there was no water. I told her that it was the upmarket suburb of Sandton near Johannesburg.

"Good. They must learn," said Ntombi. This is her usual response to many painful realities.

Ntombi then complained about the weather service predicting scattered showers, though not a drop fell. She told me it was because it was windy, as every black farmer knows. I argued that we humans broke the water system. The weather is less predictable; and climate change and mass extinctions have arrived.

"Ntombi, I will never forget how you helped me survive in Tanzania. Showing me how to make soft toilet paper by rubbing newspaper pages together; drying myself with a tiny cloth, by wringing it out and going for the next bit of skin."

Ntombi looked pleased. "With water shortage, we must go back to those things. People see a roll of toilet paper and use half the roll. How big is your arse? Three centimetres? How wet or dry is your shit today? I think about all these things when deciding how much paper I need. We used grass, stones, mud. Nobody had sores on their arses."

I had to laugh, picturing Ntombi giving a lecture to the Sandton elite on toilet paper substitutes, which I assume will include the use of designer stones.

In my retirement I look for work, paid and voluntary, that inevitably brings stress, which I seek in the way some women seem to be conditioned to seek out partners who abuse them. This annoys Ntombi, but what drives her mad is that my addiction to stress is combined with insecurity and a tail-wagging desire to please. Again, much like an abused spouse.

This creates shitty situations and I bring the shit home. This is what I once told students was the feminist "shit-eating" theory of work, which I once taught along with other theories in Sociology 101. The archetypal husband is powerless to avoid being abused by the boss, so he abuses his wife and family when he comes home to relieve the stress, thus perpetuating both patriarchy and capitalism. I saw a startled look on the faces of many of the three hundred or so students in the lecture room looking up at me. I had evidently described what they often witnessed at home.

I admire and value capitalism, provided it is somehow harnessed to the greater good, but my feeble attempts at being an entrepreneur had until then failed. Ntombi agrees I am too spineless to be good at business, but she claims I am good at patriarchy, which in theory I loathe and detest.

What Ntombi and I both agree on is that all of it is my fault, and it is true that I cannot blame either patriarchy or capitalism for my stress. She maintains that I am an evolutionary freak, lacking two of the characteristics of a mammalian male: balls and a backbone.

Reflecting on one of the more stressful situations of my pre-retirement job, I am forced to agree with Ntombi's analysis of my character. Before I retired, when I held the post of a chief director at Home Affairs, there was a senior colleague who used to push half his work onto me though I did not report to him. It had no relevance to any of the work I was paid to do. He said it would be uncomradely not to do it, and he called me "comrade" a lot . He was an excellent communicator, who had suffered much during the struggle against apartheid.

The climax came when I was persuaded to organise a massive farewell event for a minister, whom he knew I greatly respected, and who had just been appointed to a top international post. I had three weeks, and had to do everything in addition to my normal duties.

I contacted a general who knew Ntombi and borrowed the presidential ceremonial band. They agreed to spend some time with our selected officials, whose marching skills needed upgrading. I negotiated with several local schools, and they asked their children to create illustrated poems about the minister. Then I selected the best of the poems and had a leather-bound book produced. I flew down toilet cleaners and other lower-level staff the day before, who wrote and would read out statements. I persuaded a famous *mbongi* to create and sing a praise poem, and he charged the audience with amazing energies. I am sure their clients and spouses benefited for months after. The departmental choir was assembled and practised. My plan was to fill the hall with two thousand dancing, singing officials, the minister among them. All of this had to be tightly coordinated by a team of organisers whom I had put together and enthused.

On the day, the communicator asked me to shift everything by an hour because the TV crews were arriving late. Tactically, he was correct, because one strategic objective was to get our marching officials onto national news. I collapsed but stayed standing. The head of IT called to his colleagues. He was a scientifically minded man and was genuinely interested: "Hey, guys, come and look. Carneson is visibly giving off waves of stress."

I sat through the event in a stress-induced daze, and only remember one incident. I saw the minister was having trouble with her eyes. A cleaner from a remote region with a mop of wild hair had just read out a wonderful poem, and the illustrated book by schoolchildren was propped up in front of her. I asked someone from the ministry if the minister needed medical attention. She replied, "You idiot, you made her cry."

Another senior colleague, much later, had the honesty to tell me the truth. "You know when you did all that work for the head of communications? He opened two businesses over that period." Being a blabber mouth (in isiZulu they say a "wet mouth"), I complained about this injustice to Ntombi. She said, without a hint of sympathy, "You don't know your comrades yet. You are like a frog jumping into a snake's mouth. You have no balls and can never say no."

By that stage in our respective careers Ntombi had work-related stress of her own, having been promoted to the rank of lieutenant colonel in the defence force. Instead of trying to change my character and redeem myself, I gladly became the shit-eater and listened for hours to her struggles with those above and below her.

It was the least I could do. Firstly, because she had put up with my work-related stress all our married life. Secondly, we were both working for the same conflicted and shambolic government, and a degree of solidarity was in order.

I woke up one morning knowing vaguely who I was, but not knowing where I was. Scrabbling for my glasses and then for my phone, I saw that it was two o'clock and went to put on the alarm. Then I closed the "rape gate", as some paranoid white South Africans call it – the door in a passage that shuts off your sleeping quarters from the rest of the house. Gogo prods me painfully with her walking stick if I forget to lock it.

I was peckish but resisted my subconscious, which suggested that I check to see if a tap in the kitchen was running. Some years before, we had some spectacular floods when someone unknown, probably me, left a tap running in a plugged sink. Now I check every night and make sure that taps hover over unplugged sinks. My behaviour is clearly neurotic, driven by an irrational fear that hides something – in this case, a desire for a snack even though my stomach bulges over my pyjama cord.

I got under the blankets next to a mound that, with enormous relief, I identified as Ntombi. Suddenly everything was secure, rooted and comprehensible. I realised that the whole saga had happened because I had fallen into a deep sleep without getting under the bedclothes.

Recently, something in the news prompted Ntombi to say that all politicians were greedy and had "biting intestines". Her hand snaked out and she bit the air with snapping fingers. Instead of using the worn-out African phrase "politics of the stomach", she had dramatised and improved on it.

I quickly agreed, laughed, hugged her and said she had an amazing way with words. She looked suspicious, possibly because she was about to find me guilty by association. I have worked with politicians and, when I mention her weight, she likes to say, "You and your hotel finger-lunches with politicians. Look at your stomach."

Clambering over my stomach to get into bed that night, there was a small noise and the phone winked at me. No app was ticked except Facebook, which I rarely look at and do not understand. Our kids insisted that I have a page. Ntombi, by comparison, is a Facebook queen, despite being the declared enemy of modernity and wanting us all to live simple rural lives.

I touched the app, and there were comments from former colleagues whom I knew when I worked in the university sector. They are clever, decent people but they were making fun of my clan: the Recovering Workaholics. They were saying how hilarious it had been when they once contracted a bunch of retired academics to do a project. Most of the pensioned academics literally fell asleep mid-task because they were plumb wore out, as an American might have put it.

I puffed up with indignation and then deflated. The reason I was falling asleep on top of the blankets was another tough contract that I had recently signed, despite being worn out. Each of the thirteen years of my last stretch working for the government felt like ten human years. Thus, when I turn seventy soon, subjectively I will be two hundred years old. Depressed, I sent a comment: "How do you squeeze the last drop of blood from their decaying old carcases? Signed One of Them." I knew they would see my name over the comment but did not care.

As I was trying to get to sleep, I remembered that we had ended the day on a hopeful, feel-good note. South Africa had trounced the English and won the rugby World Cup, again. Saturday is the day Ntombi takes her most serious meds and they knock her out, so she had missed the match.

I had told her and Gogo that we must watch a replay of the match. We had won a victory and a good one because all kinds of South Africans had worked together. The whites provided an ace kicker and muscle, and blacks and coloureds were smart, tactical players and went for the gaps. Everybody worked cleverly together. "A Zulu?" Gogo asked and I said I thought there was one, or close enough. Ntombi had caught the highlights on the evening news, and she said what every South African was thinking: "We can do anything if we work together."

At least one in four South Africans goes to bed hungry every night, so I suggested we should start there, given there is plenty of food to go around. If we only cared enough and had leaders whose intestines did not bite.

Then I fell asleep.

Fourteen

The potions and lotions of Uncle Abel

African traditional medicine in its varied forms is holistic involving both the body and the mind. The traditional healer typically diagnoses and treats the psychological basis of an illness before prescribing medicines, particularly medicinal plants to treat the symptoms.
– M. Fawzi Mahomoodally, "Traditional Medicines in Africa", *Evidence-Based Complementary and Alternative Medicine*, 2013

JUST BEFORE COVID-19 STRUCK, Ntombi took me to visit her favourite relative, Uncle Abel Mdluli. He lives in Kwamteyi in a cluster of huts that are in various stages of breaking down. The most stable structures are two large round huts made of wood and mud bricks on top of a cement base, covered by a tin roof. One is a living space where Uncle Abel cooks, keeps his worldly goods, and seats visitors. There are also the tools of his trade, which is that of an *inyanga*, or traditional healer. *Izinyanga* mainly use remedies such as herbs. *Sangomas* are different and practise deep spiritual healing and divination.

The other hut is only for his business as an *inyanga*, on which he concentrates since he retired from his job at the factory in Johannesburg. That hut is used for making and storing traditional medicine and for treating his patients, whom I have seen lying on the grass outside.

There are two smaller structures that have four walls and a roof, but their door and window frames are struggling to keep a hold on the crumbling cement bricks. Uncle Abel sleeps in one and, when I peek through the doorway, I see a narrow bed and some heavy iron spears standing against the wall. A grandchild told me that Abel is safe alone. He is respected and feared because of his knowledge of traditions and his calling. And he still has a strong fighting arm.

Now and then Abel, or a family member, pays for a tanker to fill up a plastic water tank that sits under some trees. It drives Ntombi mad that it is not connected to a roof to harvest the rainwater. The only communal tap is about two hundred metres away, which is a long way to carry a heavy bucket. The path is too rough to make use of a wheelbarrow.

A few years ago, a small clinic was built close by, next to the tarred road. A primary school lies some distance away, over a hill, and there are no other facilities within reach. Every election a satellite police station is promised but is never delivered. The municipality has built some pit toilets, with one near Abel's supposed boundary, which he keeps clean. The pit toilet is leaning over dangerously because the ground under its concrete base is washing away.

Time washes away many things. Decades ago, when Ntombi grew up there, the homestead was full of family and had a clear boundary. They had fields nearby that produced crops and a substantial herd of goats that someone looked after for a share of the offspring. There were streams full enough and clean enough to let them drag a sack through the water and catch fish for roasting on the end of a stick.

Now the streams are polluted or dried up. Increasingly, strangers are building modern houses on the fields and commute to work in cars, or live on remittances. Of his immediate family, only Abel remains in the homestead, and people let their cows and goats roam freely on his plot. Ntombi once sent him money to put a fence around his buildings, but it was never completed and only a few posts and strands of barbed wire remain.

Uncle Abel was soon going to be ninety. He stood tall and straight and was still handsome, with regular features and skin that is quite smooth. His eyes and teeth still function, although they need attention, and his legs are getting weaker.

Abel looks around the larger valley in which Kwamteyi is situated. It stretches to the horizon, which is rimmed by hills rising to flat mountains. The valley is green in summer if it rains, and brown in winter. Within this circle he knows every visible animal and plant family, and many under the ground, including dead and living humans.

"The names of the medicines are important," he told me. "And what they mean." Abel was not referring to linguistic items of historical interest, but to the effectiveness of each medicine, which depends on its physical, spiritual and cultural properties. The names of medicines are rooted in the relationship of people to the land, to one another, and to all other living things on it. And most importantly they are rooted in people's relationship to their history and the ancestors who watch over them. He has been using this knowledge system since 1950, shortly before my own birth. He is widely respected, and *izinyanga* from other provinces sometimes consult him.

"Are there any apprentices to whom you have passed on knowledge?" I asked him.

He said nobody had been dedicated enough to do more than help him cut, pound, grind and prepare. We were sitting in his main hut, the centre of which was crowded with branches and roots and medicines in different stages of preparation. The skins and bones of jackal and snakes, feathers of guinea fowl, and quills of porcupine hung from the roof. A wooden cross and a red cloth heart with a message about love dangled among them. Perhaps a hundred bottles were scattered around the room, ranging from large brandy bottles he had emptied with his friends, to tiny flasks that once held perfume. Those in the centre of the room held medicines.

He pointed to a large branch and to the bottles of black powder to which he was reducing it. The branch weighed at least ten kilos and he may have dragged it for several kilometres through thick bush.

I told him I could not promise anything, and asked ,"Would you be willing to collaborate with medical scientists, who can harvest your knowledge? Not just what medicines are made of, and what they do, but their names and history. They would need to sign that they would respect your right to your own knowledge, and perhaps pay you as a researcher."

"I would very much like that, but first I must organise my medicines."

Abel got up and I followed him into the other large hut, his medicine store and factory. I had never seen inside, as he always kept the door closed. We entered and I saw that the rough concrete floor was covered with thousands of bottles, many filled with medicine.

"What I need, John, is shelving. As it is, how can my customers have confidence in me? With shelves and labels, it would look professional. I may even put on a white coat. The stock would be organised, and I would do much more business."

Ntombi supported the idea, and so began the saga of Uncle Abel's shelving and related matters. One matter was his need for glasses so that he could read labels and he agreed to go to an optician in Ladysmith. It would be his first eye examination of any kind, and I set it up for the following week. Unfortunately, the Covid-19 pandemic struck, a lockdown was announced, and he did not go.

We were on a four-day visit, expressly to see Uncle Abel, and I was sharing a self-catering family room in a guest house in Ladysmith with Ntombi and Gogo. Although she had memories of slaving for his family, she had always liked and respected Abel, her most senior *mkhwenyana*, or brother-in-law.

On our last morning we scoured the large stores for new shelving and managed to get the last pack of three shelves to take to him, with a box of tools. A worker at the guest house gave us the name of a shop owned by Indians which had second-hand shelving. Ladysmith has hardly been decolonised, and although the shop was close by, it was in an area hardly ever visited by whites.

We had been warned that shops were closing because of civil unrest against corruption and the ANC mayor, led by drivers of trucks and minibus taxis who might block the roads. We drove past largely empty blocks of shops and street markets, including a street with a market dedicated to African traditional medicine, and managed to find the shop we had been told about.

The shopkeepers were part of a well-established Indian family and they could organise transport. We negotiated with one of the senior family members, who arrived after a phone call. The price was relatively high, and we decided against buying the shelves. Without us there to find suitable workers and supervise the delivery and reconstruction, too much could go wrong.

The next day, before we left for Pretoria, we dropped off the small set of shelves and a box of tools, and said goodbye to Uncle Abel. The police and lorry drivers were putting up their respective roadblocks, and we were lucky to get through to the highway.

I managed to send Abel a larger set of shelves after many complications. I finally understood that the delivery company was reluctant to go to Kwamteyi. It was not on Google maps, and they claimed that trucks had been hijacked in the area. I stated, sincerely, that I felt safer there than I did in Pretoria.

The other matter I tried to follow up was to interest a research unit in working with Uncle Abel to harvest his medical and cultural knowledge. My first step was to phone someone senior I knew at the Medical Research Council and ask how seriously such research was being taken. The answer was that the two specialised units responsible for traditional medicine in the council and the ministry had been closed and their functions discontinued or absorbed. It proved impossible, given the lockdown, to get a response to my calls and emails from the management of medical research teams at several universities.

I saw a headline in the media that the national organisation representing traditional healers had lodged an official complaint with the Minister of Health about being left out of the national effort to combat the coronavirus. A few million rand was put aside, and a project initiated to investigate the efficacy of traditional medicine in treating patients recovering from Covid-19. The thought of getting Abel through layers of finely crafted bureaucracy and patronage made me feel sick.

I remembered that the master who, with his wife, teaches me t'ai chi is a doctor of Chinese medicine. He has treated me for a joint problem with acupuncture, massage, and herbal pills and poultices. He had years before diagnosed Ntombi's thrombosis and treated it before South African doctors could diagnose it; and he had successfully treated a pinched nerve in our daughter Busi's shoulder. An internet search revealed that in China traditional medicine has been researched and standardised and has been proved to speed up recovery from Covid-19.

My conclusion was that I would have to disappoint Uncle Abel. It seemed to me that many things in South Africa needed to be decolonised, besides the town Ladysmith. The town was named after the wife of Sir Harry Smith, who has two other towns named after him. An ardent racist, he once forced a captured African chief to lie down so he could put a booted foot on his neck.

For Ntombi, the destruction of the environment mirrors the erosion of the family and its values. She sees Uncle Abel as one of the last foundation stones holding up her family. Even in exile, she tried to strengthen that foundation and save the house for future generations. She sometimes sent money or goods and often warnings, encouragement and advice.

Uncle Abel told me that it was a great pity Ntombi had been born a woman, as she would have been able to lead and support the family. I disagreed with him for several reasons, but kept quiet. Ntombi, when sufficiently angry, grabs her breasts and says, "These are my balls and I do more with them than these useless men can do with the little things they hang about them."

Nomvula and Ntombi often tell me that it was Abel's money that kept them alive, as they received little from her husband Shoti, who liked to dress fashionably. Both men had been migrant workers in Johannesburg, not seeing their families for eleven months of the year.

Abel gave Shoti money for shoes and clothing, among other things, which assisted him to establish himself in exile in Swaziland after he abandoned Nomvula and her two children. He continues to do what he can to help his remaining family, even as his homestead crumbles around him.

Ntombi spends hours on the phone reminding relatives of everything Abel has done to assist them and listing all the things he needs help with. She tells them that even while struggling in exile, she had sent money to help support Abel and other family members. Her efforts have resulted in some of Abel's grandchildren assisting him regularly.

You may want to know if the shelves have been assembled and if labelled bottles are being organised in a way that reflects Uncle Abel's knowledge system. We heard that one of the grandchildren promised to put up the shelves when he got a chance. After Covid restrictions were relaxed, we paid a visit to Abel, a five-hour drive away. Ntombi assembled the shelves herself, with some inept attempts by me to help her.

Fifteen
The Gupta, Gupta spin cycle

If they can get you asking the wrong questions, they don't have to worry about answers.
– Thomas Pynchon, *Gravity's Rainbow*, 1973

WRITING ABOUT MY LIFE, I realised that I have always been fascinated by shifts in social consciousness, which is at the core of the story of the Buddha. He was protected by the king, his father, from knowledge of death and disease, and believed that a pleasant life of luxury was the whole of reality. One day he saw a man dying of a dreadful illness, and someone explained the facts of life to him.

At one time many people thought that John Vorster, Hitler, Stalin and the local bishop were infallible and could do no wrong. I am referring, respectively, to the majority of white South Africans, Hitler Youth, Young Communists and parents of choirboys. When the veil of illusion is lifted there is denial, bewilderment and, for some, enlightenment. Before the enlightenment, there is often fear and paranoia, as reality in general becomes shaky and even menacing.

Every day, for over a year, Deputy Chief Justice Raymond Zondo's commission has been hearing testimony about how critical parts of our state were captured by a cabal led by a wealthy Indian family, the Guptas. Among the captured institutions were the revenue service, the police, the prosecuting authority, state intelligence, the broadcasting authority, government ministries, major state enterprises, and so on. Ntombi and I and millions of other citizens were avid viewers of the Commission's televised proceedings.

The direct loss of resources to corruption over the ten years of the last two administrations is conservatively estimated by our new head of the prosecuting authority to be R1.4 trillion or nearly a $100 billion. Indirectly, the costs have been much higher. Firstly, state capture involved the systematic destruction of institutions by replacing key managers with crooks or incompetents, who had no interest in good governance, planning, maintenance or development. Secondly, it created a climate of fear and hopelessness. Thirdly, populist racial nationalism, crafted by British public relations company Bell Pottinger, was used to undermine values rooted in centuries of struggle.

All of this has a profound influence on our little household and on the country, on our relationships, well-being, mental states, security and material conditions. More than ten per cent of the value of the fund that guarantees our pensions was wiped out by those operating the shadow state and by large multinational corporations such as Steinhoff and PricewaterhouseCoopers that were complicit or took advantage of the destruction of state controls.

I picture the former president Jacob Zuma hiding in the bell tower of a large cathedral, deaf to the pleas of the people. He sits down at a gigantic organ. The first notes – the sustained high notes that run through horror movie scores – unsettle and destabilise one of his target organisations. Accusations and rumours increase in volume, amplified by social media and by the Gupta-owned TV channel and national newspaper. An atmosphere of insecurity is created and amplified by secret social media laboratories.

The organist plays on the fears the people have for their jobs, families and safety. Those that oppose what is happening are dismissed with fake charges, and the rest of the staff are too afraid to speak up. Many tell the Zondo Commission about devastated lives, death threats and nervous breakdowns.

The organist begins to furiously work the pedals and stops as he combines the themes of insecurity and fear. Then his hand rises and falls dramatically, and he hits the paranoia key. This is the deepest of all notes, a persistent rumble that confuses you and clouds your judgement. You will start to doubt everything you believe in and mistrust everyone, including yourself.

Almost every day violent arguments erupt in our house as Ntombi and I respond to the news that comes out of our TV, radios, cell phones and computers. Gogo retreats to her room or sits quietly at the table. Ntombi mocks me for blaming all our troubles on Zuma and the Guptas, like a typical white who is blind to the systemic looting of white monopolists. I shout that this charge was planted by Bell Pottinger and others hired by the Zuptas.

I realised that Ntombi's accusation of obsession was justified when I found myself mesmerised by the washing machine. When it hit the spin cycle, all I could hear was "Gupta, gupta, gupta".

I start yelling about the shadow state and hidden media labs churning out fake news; about the billions looted that could have funded the new national health system or been used to invest in the new economy and create jobs. She tells me I am working myself up to a heart attack, her tone was far from sympathetic. She suggests my energy would be put to better use by helping her in the house and the garden. She blames our problems on the whole ANC being corrupt, starting with Nelson Mandela doing a deal with white capitalists.

I had to admit that there was much truth in what she was saying. We discovered we have strongly held values that we share, and that we agreed on what must be done. There is sweetness and light, and peace descends on us like a soft blanket. That is, until one or both of us are outraged by another item on the news, and then the cycle starts again, each time a little more violent.

Despite the troubling times, we gradually seem to be building a common understanding; although on the way we often revert to violent arguments. One reason is that everything we think, feel and say is an echo of a national conversation that is going on. I hear it in the voices of callers on the radio and in the pitter-patter of talk show hosts and the people they interview.

There is another reason, to which a mountain of evidence points, from various commissions. The violent struggle for control of the state is heating up as the shadow state continues to operate and mobilise people based on racial ideologies. They sabotage the justice system and the economy, and systematically undermine their opponents in the government and state to produce desperation and chaos.

It is good that for the first time many of us are hearing on national media the views of rural people, taxi drivers, housewives, and people who are homeless. Like us, they are angry and insecure. People are applying their minds and doing research. They quote facts and stats about the cost of fraud and corruption. Perhaps the internet is more empowering than confusing and disempowering.

One Friday, events unfolded that convinced me that fear and paranoia have the upper hand and have messed up my head, and that of the nation. Around ten Ntombi got up and I started preparing for a class that I attend at a university. I collected the documents I needed and found my wallet and car keys.

Ntombi was watching the funeral of a man who was supposed to give evidence at the State Capture Commission. He was not connected with the state capture process, but his company had scored many billions' worth of dodgy tenders through bribes and doing favours for ANC leaders and politicians. The day before the hearing he held a prayer meeting at his head office and booked out a small company car, leaving his BMW X5. I and others suspect he deliberately drove his small car at high speed into the side of a bridge, and he was killed.

The funeral service consisted of a series of eulogies by family members and ANC politicians about all the good he had done in the days of the struggle, defying the apartheid government, and helping comrades and black sport and businesses. Ntombi noted that it is a mistake not to acknowledge the good people have done. I exploded with outrage like a frog puffed up to the size of a giant watermelon.

After many angry words were shouted up and down the corridor, Ntombi's last remark to me as I rushed to the car were, "You are going to have that heart attack. Anytime soon." I tried, and failed, to detect a note of concern in her voice. Shaking with anger, I threw my bag into the boot and reversed out of the garage.

There was a large man walking towards a neighbour's house with a piece of paper in his hand whom I noted but did not worry about. As I turned the corner, I failed to find my mobile phone. I decided it was better to go back, park in the garage and check if the phone was still in the bag. A few hours earlier a woman had been robbed at gunpoint nearby by men cruising around in a new Mercedes. Still angry and not thinking straight, I parked outside the garage, opened the garage door halfway, went into the boot, grabbed the bag, dashed in, closed the door, and checked the bag. The phone was there.

I glanced up at a screen in the garage connected to my security cameras. Not only had I left my car door wide open, but the large man, still holding his piece of paper, was now across the road, looking at my car. I grabbed a weapon, which I keep propped up next to the door. My children sometimes park outside when they visit, and the razor-sharp cane knife is meant to defend them if they are attacked. In my imagination a hijacker is pointing a gun at them through his window, and I rush out to disarm the hijacker using a backward circular sweep.

I opened the garage door and dashed out, holding the phone. The video shows a small old man with a shiny bald head. He is shaking with fear and holds a carbon-steel machete. There is no sound, but the conversation went like this:

"Do not cross the road. I am standing exactly where they hijacked me and pointed a gun at my ten-year-old son." This was true and I still have flashbacks when standing outside the garage. Sipho and I had been forced to lie down there.

"Boss, I am coming over. I am just looking for work."

"You see that corner? Just down that road a woman was robbed at gunpoint this morning."

"Boss, look at my face." His complexion was light, and he was telling me he was not black and therefore not a danger. He started crossing the road. He was tall and fit, with broad shoulders.

"I do not care about your face. Come closer and I will blow your fucking head off." I was screaming now and reached inside the car. He hesitated, not knowing what I might be reaching for.

"Boss, what you are doing is not right. I will lay charges." But he stepped back, and I drove off. He was probably casing houses by pretending to look for work when nobody was at home, so he was not going to lay charges. He had the manner of someone in command, so he would likely send youngsters to do the robberies or hijackings.

These events explain why, because of my messed-up head, I arrived at the university with a machete in the car and my pile of notes forgotten in my garage.

Over the weekend various forms of violence escalated across the country. Many trucks were torched by local drivers angry that they were driven by foreigners. Criminal gangs used anti-foreigner sentiment as an excuse to loot and burn shops in Johannesburg. It was Women's Month, aimed at raising consciousness about femicide, and the brutal killing of several women made national news. The drivers of fleets of minibus taxis threatened to wage war on drug dealers in the centre of Pretoria. A six-year-old girl child was snatched from outside her school and held for ransom – an unusual crime in South Africa. A teacher appeared to be involved.

That night, Ntombi and I watched the news in silence, holding hands.

Fear of the state capture network continued to confound me.

A week later I got up at five to do some work and have an early breakfast. First, I turned off the alarm system and switched on the lights to scare away petty thieves who like to drop in on our neighbourhood at that time.

I took a selfie using a faux-gold mirror, having cooked and eaten a cheese omelette. A long golden hair hung from my chin, and I stared at it until realising it was a strand of cheese. Then I remembered that not long after midnight on the previous day, I had woken Ntombi because I suspected there was an attempted coup d'état by state capture forces.

Firstly, the internet suddenly went down, causing me to lose an hour of my work. Secondly, I discovered the landline and the two wireless networks we use for our data and mobile phones were dead. I switched on the radio and TV and then rushed to my car to check the commercial stations. Nothing alarming was on national or international news channels, but Ntombi pointed out most of the local programmes were recordings at that hour.

Without internet there was no way to check on what was happening or coordinate anything. And if I could phone, who would we trust enough? In a coup, this can be a life-saving or life-threatening question.

Suddenly there was a total power blackout, relieved only by distant street lights and office blocks with generators. To check this, I clambered up the iron staircase to the flat we built above our garage, which we rent out.

We are used to power cuts, the crooks who ran and still run a shadow state having looted the energy agency after building coal power stations at treble the planned cost, which work at half the planned capacity. They neglected maintenance programmes, by sacking honest people and appointing those who were focused on thieving and arranging more corrupt tenders.

Our solar power system had not kicked in and I wondered, insanely, if the gangsters had found a way to sabotage it, as it is connected to the internet. I waited for the dawn so I could set up our own generator to charge the batteries. I was seething with paranoia, as an irritated Ntombi observed. My hands were shaking.

Gogo, Ntombi's mother, was wise and stayed under the covers in her bedroom.

The networks and power were restored after a couple of hours. A growling Ntombi discovered that I had sabotaged our solar system by accidentally connecting a heater and draining the batteries. We learned by WhatsApp from our excellent neighbourhood watch captain that cable theft had caused blackouts in several suburbs, which I assumed had disrupted the networks.

An angry man even more paranoid than I was, suspected sabotage and asked on social media if this was perhaps a practice move against the state. As I was reading his tweet, a newsreader told me about an attempted coup in Ethiopia, apparently instigated by those who do not like moves to reduce corruption. One of the counter-measures taken was to shut down the internet.

I took my paranoid ass back to bed as Ntombi got up to start her day. Soon she was muttering loudly that I had left dirty dishes in the sink – and quite rightly pointing out that once again I had forgotten to clean the mirror after shaving, like the dirty, spoilt white man that I was. I decided to get my paranoia under control, before anxiety, panic attacks and other symptoms disabled me.

A few months later, in July 2022, there was an actual move against the state and the economy. After months of violence against trucks on key roads, and a week after the former President was jailed for contempt of the Constitutional Court, two thousand shopping malls and factories were looted and burned down and infrastructure attacked. There were over three hundred deaths and at least forty billion dollars' worth of damage and hundred and thirty-thousand jobs lost. Over twenty thousand businesses were destroyed, most of them owned by black people who had paid for them in blood and sweat.

Nobody has gone to jail yet for planning and coordinating the attacks, although yet another inquiry found evidence, and concluded that the security and justice systems were paralysed by conflicts within the ANC. Then, while completing this book, arsonists burnt down much of our Parliament, a beautiful historic building where I had spent many days while working for government.

I have decided some situations are too serious for me to waste time being paranoid.

Sixteen

Marie Kondo and the apocalypse

A fresh approach to decluttering based on a spiritual relationship with one's possessions.
– Marie Kondo, *The Life-Changing Magic of Tidying Up*, 2014

Once we got used to level two of the Covid lockdown, we began to be nostalgic for level four, when you were not allowed beyond your house and garden without a special permit. If you had internet and enough space, money and resources, this could be a novel and pleasant experience for a few weeks or even longer. Many discovered that they worked twice as efficiently at home and could plug into the digital economy and make more money.

In our house at least, we found that we enjoyed being with one another and began to do things together, such as talk about the past, cook, and work in the garden. At one stage we thought we should lock down every year, just as some people fast periodically for various reasons. What I loved most was the opportunity to share something of value that we saw in different ways and to explore what we have in common. It might be discussing a friend or a film or a country.

One such occasion happened after we had moved to level two of the lockdown and Busi had gone back to Johannesburg. One evening she phoned us.

"Look up this Netflix show: *Tidying with Marie Kondo*."

Dubious but curious, we watched Marie Kondo that evening while sitting up in bed. Ntombi was all for it, since it was a reality show and she thought cleanliness was better than godliness. Also, it was impossible to resist Marie Kondo, the tidying lady. She glows with spiritual strength and joy when she enters and then kneels and thanks your house for allowing her in. Ntombi was fascinated.

"Ah, so the Japanese do it. Just like we do. You know how our houses are built in a line, from north to south. In the old days you could not just go to the back of the houses, where we kept the kraal for animals. That is where my grandfather walked from one end to the other when visitors arrived from Johannesburg, calling the ancestors to welcome them. You can be a Christian, but you must do the rituals and connect with the ancestors. Just like that Marie woman."

I spent the rest of the evening learning how to fold my underpants, drilled military-style by retired Lieutenant Colonel Ntombi. She told me, "Open like a butterfly, fold over like birds' wings. Turn it so and the label will look at you. See how neatly they line up. Like soldiers. Do that one again."

We both knew that my tidy drawer would soon be disrupted by entropy, the inevitable descent of the universe into lazy chaos, which Ntombi blames on me. Ntombi's tolerance of my weakness is not limitless, and I have a well-founded fear of my underclothes being tossed like refugees into a bin or the street.

Pleased with the Marie Kondo experience the previous night, the following evening I decided to bring Ntombi a special film neither of us had seen. I handed her an old DVD of a film in its original cover, a 1953 iconic cowboy movie, painted bright in Technicolor, which revolves around a war over land between small farmers and a cattle rancher. I had months before spotted the DVD in a second-hand shop. The movie was *Shane*, based on a 1949 novel that was one of a set that Ntombi had to study for her Junior Certificate in Swaziland.

Ntombi often mentions her school set books: *Shane*, *The Radium Woman* and *Shaka Zulu*. She always jumps up and shows how her teacher, Mrs Kgabede, despite being elderly, would make the books come alive by acting them out. Mrs Kgabede would spring into the air, then whip out two imaginary guns or crouch by a desk. Or she would be a thundering Shaka, telling his massed regiments that any soldier who returned with wounds on his back would be executed. The books would be read out aloud, with Ntombi sitting in a large group that had a printed copy.

We settle down to watch the film, which was much better than I expected. Towards the end, the rancher sends his thugs to terrorise the homesteaders who share the beautiful valley with him. One family wants to up and leave. They are looking at their hogs feeding in their pen and one explains to a neighbour, "They killed the sow."

As Shane headed for his showdown with the rancher and his thugs, Ntombi interrupted my thoughts and the film, and said, "It would be good to keep pigs." She explained she was thinking of the land her grandfather had farmed before it was seized and given to white farmers. When she was a child, he kept pigs which got fat on leftovers from harvests and the kitchen.

Ntombi told me, "We have a saying in Zulu that a traveller has a stomach like a bird, meaning any food would be welcome to them. You were blessed if you gave them some grains and sugar for energy. Any *makoti* – a young wife – would step aside and bow to an older stranger they met on the road. There was respect and real *ubuntu*. That has all gone with the land that was grabbed from us. People were poor, but they walked far and ate healthy food."

I asked her where she was when her mother's family was forcibly removed.

"I was already in exile. I heard people discussing those big army trucks taking people by force from Ekuphumuleni, and dumping them on the open veld at Zakheni, a place far away. They lost most of their belongings. Imagine you were at work and the children were at home. They removed the children and just knocked down the walls. Unless you were there, you may have empathy, but you will not feel the pain."

Being reminded of the horrors of apartheid , and having our state captured and then being attacked by Covid-19, was not enough to make me see visions of an apocalypse. It took Donald Trump to do that, with his pronouncements on nuclear war. Even then, I would normally require the assistance of alcohol to see visions, but buying liquor was banned under stage one lockdown in South Africa.

This pleased Ntombi, as did the ban on the sale of cigarettes. Gogo stayed neutral. I do not smoke, but I warned her of the consequences of the prohibition of alcohol in the United States: the illicit sale and drinking of poisonous brews, and the rise in crime and political corruption. The illegal cigarette trade in South Africa was already a large-scale criminal enterprise, connected to state capture. Ntombi listened carefully, but her joy in prohibiting something she dislikes overcame logic. I kept quiet. I have many little pleasures and am allowed misbehaviours that may be at risk if I do not stay silent at sensitive moments.

One sin was having an occasional tot of liquor. Here the logic and facts were on her side, as I knew people, including me, would be more careless if we had any intoxicating substances. The most urgent need was to keep limited ICU beds for Covid-19 victims and not for victims of violence and drunken drivers. After the ban on alcohol there was a large drop in emergency cases being admitted to hospitals.

The personal consumption of alcohol was legal but risky, and I did not think it ethical or wise to drink any liquor that might be on our property. However, the parallels between the continuing injustices in South Africa and the movie were enough to drive me to drink. We were indeed killing the sow by allowing our greedy elites, white and black, to trash our new state. I went to look for a bottle in our lapa by the pool. In the back of the drinks cabinet, I found some fruit juice and something labelled Cape to Rio, pure cane spirit, triple distilled.

I took my concoction around the side of the house to the TV room, avoiding the kitchen where Ntombi was cooking a species of semi-wild spinach she had collected in the garden. We both call it *mchicha*, the Kiswahili word for the plant, instead of *imbuya* the isiZulu word for the African varieties that Ntombi grows from seeds as fine as stardust.

Viva spinach and its promoter Popeye – the cartoon is so popular in South Africa that in township slang all animated films to this day are called "popeyes". Archaeological research tells us that semi-wild spinach was a staple before the colonial invasion. It was packed with vitamins and roughage. Khoisan hunters and gatherers made sure the seeds were broadcast in a damp place before they moved on, chasing the herds of antelope that were sensing the rains. They returned to the exact spot months later. The latest discoveries show that their culture may be forty thousand years old, based on carbon-dating of tools.

Sprawling on a couch in the TV room, alcoholic drink in hand, I selected a cool-looking Netflix film *Sound and Fury* by Sturgill Simpson. The credits said, "In this anime visual album, a mysterious driver heads deep into a postapocalyptic hellscape towards a ferocious showdown with two monstrous opponents."

It did not mention that the opponents looked like a male and female version of Trump. In the animated movie, I imagined I saw, or did see, a sweet child, innocent face upturned, asking the question, "Daddy, what was there before the a-pop-o-lips?" Her father was looking out of the window at a city that could have been Cape Town, where I was born, blasted by nuclear strikes and half drowned by the rising sea, with twisted skyscrapers strewn about, humped like caterpillars.

There is no answer. Her father keeps quiet, and tears stream down his scarred face. The cane spirit kicked in, and my mind started wandering and wondering. Maybe the remnant of the Khoisan, also known as the Bushmen, will be the only survivors of the a-pop-o-lips. A few have survived smallpox, wars of extermination, forced labour, and recruitment into the apartheid army to track down ANC and SWAPO fighters. We need their survival skills, like yesterday.

Shoals of visual tropes swam across the screen, fished out of our global cultural stew by Sturgill and five Japanese guest directors. The heroes wore samurai armour and hi-tech goggles and carried two swords. I studied their technique, having recently started using the Chinese straight sword in t'ai chi. Compilations of heavy metal country rock pounded away.

It was a blast and, indeed, the art form for our age and the coming apocalypses. If we survive, perhaps Sturgill Simpson will pay us a visit. We could relax on the three couches lining the walls of our TV room, while Marie Kondo brought us tidy cocktails and plumped the cushions.

Seventeen
John remembers his screams

Screams might seem simple, but they can actually convey a complex set of emotions. The arsenal of human screams has been honed over millions of years of evolution, with subtle nuances in volume, timing and inflection that can signal different things.
– Frank T. McAndrew, "Why We Love Blood-Curdling Screams", *Live Science*, 2019

As you become deafer, your brain fills in what your ears do not catch. You imagine, for example, that somebody calls you and you drive your spouse mad with, "Did you call me, my turtle dove?" No answer, so you trot down the corridor to the kitchen where she is fixing an appliance with a look of fierce concentration. You know that look, and wait. She eventually notices you and snaps, "What do you want?" And you ask if she had called you, to which the standard reply is, "It is so annoying when you interrupt me. Put on your hearing aid."

I remembered that when my father was going deaf, he would tell my mother, "Do you know what it feels like to stick a foreign object in your ear?" I usually do not reply but retreat with as much dignity as I can find.

Now and again, I panic when I imagine hearing somebody scream. I am much deafer in one ear, so I am never sure where a sound comes from and rush around the house trying to pick up the sound again. Then I turn on the two-way radio linked to the Neighbourhood Watch to check if a scream is being discussed. It never is, and I conclude it was a rusty hinge or a car tyre squealing.

One night, Ntombi was brushing her teeth in the bathroom and remarked, "Some kids are fucking, again. Now they are arguing." It was the kind of thing she would not usually say, so I considered some possibilities. A couple of drunks could not restrain themselves, but we were in Covid lockdown, and nobody walks our streets that late at night, drunk or sober. Homeless people could not be guilty, as they have been settled in tents on the sports fields around our t'ai chi club, forcing us to prop up our tablets and learn online.

It was possible that Ntombi was hearing something from a house one hundred metres away which had teenagers, but even when her senses are sharpened by a migraine, that is a stretch. They held occasional parties, but no large party could be held during any phase of the lockdown. I was forced to conclude that the new tenant of our garden flat had brought a girlfriend home. I suggested this to her.

"Are you mad? I said that cats are fucking and making noise. Go put on your hearing aid."

Ntombi chased me out of her tiny bathroom. She was still listening to the neighbour's cats. I could not hear anything, but she could identify each one by their yowl, knew which house they called home, and how much shit each had deposited on her seedlings. She was no doubt comparing the cats' mating habits with those of their humans. Attributing collective guilt and distributing punishment is Ntombi's thing, and I shuddered.

As it was a Saturday, I had found Gogo in our bedroom that evening watching a programme of traditional African dancing and singing. The room was filled with a compelling rhythm, a lead singer who was middle-aged and fit, and young women responding with harmony and grace. I tried to follow, hoping not to complicate my foot, knee and back problems.

Gogo encouraged me, saying, "Bheka lo, Fred and Sarah, umfana ga wena dansa kumnandi." She was calling on the shades of my parents to see how nicely their boy was dancing.

I later thought about screams and Gogo. The one time I heard a horrific scream in our house it had come from her room, usually an oasis of peace and quiet. It was three in the morning and the hairs on the back of my neck stood up, individually and severally. Ntombi was out of bed and moving towards the door before I could decide what to do. I heard voices and she came back. She explained that Gogo had been woken by her dead sister, and went back to bed. We had been informed of the death of her sister in Ladysmith the day before. Gogo had been very close to her sisters when she lived in Ladysmith and still misses them more than any other aspect of her life there.

That night in bed, I remembered two other occasions when unexpected screams had electrified me.

I was teaching English in Lisbon in 1978, after the pro-democracy coup that ended a fifty-year-old fascist regime. One day I was seated in a cinema next to a Portuguese friend watching the Italian film *Novecento*. On the screen a left-wing activist was being beaten to death by Mussolini's thugs. A man seated in front of us rose and screamed loudly enough to drown the soundtrack, the city, the world. It was a repeated phrase like "*Pare com isso, bastardos*." My friend said calmly, "Ah, one of the tortured."

The other occasion took place in the centre of Pretoria in the 1990s. I was with an extraordinary woman I will call Cassie. She frazzled my nerves worse than her hair, which was demented, with her wild black eyes moving all over a thin, white face. I had been seconded to lead a team developing part of the new school curriculum and was told to work with a consultant they had hired.

She told me that afternoon, "We are going to see a deputy director-general," as if we were Catholics being presented to a cardinal. In the meeting she viciously attacked me for being a reactionary. I had argued for a well-structured curriculum, saying that the British Empire was run efficiently by officials who had learned Latin and Greek. The DDG smiled and said mildly, "Cassie, I think John was making a general point."

Cassie asked me to walk with her to her car, which was a reasonable request considering we were in the back streets of Pretoria and it was early evening. We were parked in side streets, on opposite sides of a six-lane road. There was nobody around and I said, "Look, I think it is OK, you go across and shout if you need me."

I watched her cross and turned to go and find my car. There was a scream as if from the mouth of hell and, without thinking, I sprinted across the road. A muscle in my calf tore when I was halfway across, and for a moment I was certain I had been shot. I dragged myself to the gutter and a smiling Cassie looked down at me. "I thought I saw something near my car."

I had to wear an orthopaedic boot and use crutches for three months. Later I learned that the apartheid regime had given Cassie a hard time. I am sure that was true and that she also gave her comrades a hard time. Sometimes, despite my best efforts, I think reactionary and inhumane thoughts.

Memories of Cassie disturbed me, which was risky. I would have troubled sleep or no sleep. I decided to think through a t'ai chi drill and then recall the walk I had taken around five in the afternoon, within the time allocated for walks under that level of Covid-19 regulations.

All walks at that time in the Highveld are magic, whether in Johannesburg or a game park. The sky becomes solid, a light-blue jelly you want to cut and watch as it peels back to reveal stars. It is the colour of jeans – not those washed and torn in a factory to make a fashion statement, but the ones that hugged the thighs of Janis Joplin singing, "And I's feelin' near as faded as my jeans."

The world grows flatter and quieter. I recalled that President Paul Kruger, before throwing his people under the British imperial omnibus, employed experts to prove that the world was flat. Even the birds were quiet, and perhaps Oom Paul, taking his walk, would whistle one of their tunes. He could imitate the calls of more than one hundred species, and black Africans called him Ma Melodi, wrongly supposed by some to be the origin of the name of the township of a similar name.

On Saturdays Gogo always used to give me a few rands in a little plastic bag with her Lotto tickets. She hardly ever wins and even then the amount is small. But it matters not. I would exchange a few words with the lady in the Portuguese corner shop. "Como está a minha senhora? Tudo bem?"

It reminded me of the way the South African author Herman Charles Bosman felt about marches. He wrote that he loved to join any march, not caring where it was going or why. He liked being part of a column of humanity marching forward, and it was best when tramping through a persistent rain. Gogo did not know why, but she was ever hopeful that she would win enough money to share her wealth among her grandchildren. I walked back home through a soft light which was fading fast, the sky turning a blue-black.

I had fallen asleep and Ntombi woke me up to warn me not to snore. I thought through my t'ai chi moves to get back to sleep. You do not just walk in t'ai chi. You move forward to attack very slowly and gently, knees bent. You sweep one hand up to the level of a throat, I assume to cut it. The other hand sweeps across in a move called "brush knee" and ends up guarding your vitals. Every step back is an organised retreat, heel of the hand slowly extended to push back the enemy. I was finding that organising thoughts and memories into stories was a bit like that, going back and forth over an idea or a decade, guardedly.

Amused by my own thinking, a depressing reminder that I am old, I picked up my phone and scrolled through the messages. On our family WhatsApp group there was a photo from Ntombi containing an advert for Incontinence Underwear. There was no message.

The next morning, before Ntombi woke up, I hurried to make sure I had mopped around my toilet and did my laundry. I first carefully inserted new hearing aids into my ears. They were adjustable and I worked the tiny buttons to increase their sensitivity. She likes to creep up and surprise me when I am daydreaming instead of doing my chores. It would not happen again.

Eighteen

Ntombi and the secrets of the pool

Water is fluid, soft and yielding. But water will wear away rock, which is rigid and cannot yield. As a rule, whatever is fluid, soft and yielding will overcome whatever is rigid and hard. This is another paradox: what is soft is strong.
– Lao Tzu, Chinese philosopher and reputed author of *Tao Te Ching*

SOMETIMES, WHEN I COME across Ntombi's dress uniform hanging in a cupboard, I feel like saluting, although I have never been a soldier. She is now retired but in theory can be mobilised and may have to attend ceremonies. I am not sure how these things work, but I think she will be buried in her uniform.

Ntombi had always wanted to join the army, and when young she was active in the front line of the armed struggle as a courier and supervisor of safe houses. In exile she acquired advanced catering and housekeeping skills and qualifications. Soldiers in the new South African defence force are no different from any other, and love to eat and sleep.

When we settled near Pretoria in early 2001, Ntombi applied for work in the army. We spent many hours filling out forms, writing CVs and asking the police to stamp copies of her qualifications. After a year of fruitless effort Ntombi began to visit offices and use exile contacts to check on what was happening. We discovered that there was a three-way war in the army, between people historically from the armies of the African National Congress (ANC), the Pan Africanist Congress (PAC), and the army of the former apartheid state. They were all skilled manipulators of human resources and logistics, but the Afrikaners knew the systems best. Some had been finagling posts and stealing long before the first democratic election in 1994.

Ntombi's applications were binned, and her certificates stolen, the first few times by a member of the PAC, who later had the grace to apologise. She assumed Ntombi was white because she used her married name, being proud of her father-in-law Fred Carneson, who was a veteran of the ANC army, Umkhonto we Sizwe. She even knows his soldier's number from the Second World War.

ANC members then "lost" other applications, driven by the belief that she was white, or was married to a white, and that any vacant post belonged by right to their private networks of comrades, relatives and friends. Ntombi was forced to use her own network in defence, and senior officers eventually intervened. She had valuable qualifications and experience and obtained a temporary post as a captain in the reserve force. They put her in charge of catering services at a military hospital, which had a kitchen staffed by forty workers and was badly in need of attention.

On her first day in charge of the hospital kitchens, Captain Ntombi came across a locked door. Her Afrikaner subordinate told her not to worry about that little room. "Then fetch a key," Ntombi ordered. Excuse after excuse was given until Ntombi told her to bring "one of those fat hammers". They both knew she meant a sledgehammer, but neither knew the word in English. Ntombi speaks no Afrikaans, and the Afrikaner did not speak isiZulu.

A key was produced and Ntombi unlocked the door. It was a terrible sight. There were cosy armchairs around a table with flowers, family photos, lace doilies and dainty teacups. The three white staff were keeping thirty-five black staff out of the staff kitchenette.

Ntombi cared little for rank or military protocol and made up her own operational policy, which roughly coincided with that of the Constitution. The kitchen was there to produce and deliver food that would boost morale and get sick or injured soldiers fit again as soon as possible. She was relentless in pursuit of this goal and often chased away generals who were used to being served a cup of tea and a plate of scrambled eggs.

Ntombi got her hands dirty, showing staff the proper way to clean a pot or a machine, and fought corruption. For example, she turned away consignments of food that were substandard. She waved slabs of fat in the faces of suppliers and lectured them on heart disease, and she tightened control of the stores. She walked around the wards every day to talk to patients and responded to complaints.

She was later promoted to major, and remained in the reserve for years, when she should have been absorbed into the permanent force. Once it was known who she was, she was deftly blocked by Afrikaner bureaucrats, who tried to keep control of posts, as well as by members of former liberation movements who worked their own patronage networks.

Because of the war in the army, we decided to go to war with the army. We spent many hours writing letters that documented what had happened. We got lawyers to threaten legal action, appending evidence, and Ntombi was finally made a member of the permanent force.

Her eventual rank was that of lieutenant colonel, after a direct battle for the post with an Afrikaner woman, who was supported by white administrators. Once again, Ntombi's files were lost, and we had to resort to lawyers before the matter was resolved. The

Afrikaner woman later received her promotion elsewhere and became one of Ntombi's friends and allies.

The damage by then had been done. Ntombi was left with nine years until retirement and therefore did not qualify to receive a monthly pension and other benefits. Her health had begun to deteriorate, so her most productive years were over when she could have done much more in the permanent force.

Crucial medical benefits were eventually secured by Ntombi as she was a military veteran because of her work on the front line in the depths of the anti-apartheid struggle. That victory took hundreds of hours of our battling a dysfunctional and corrupt bureaucracy. It was at the height of state capture, when South Africa was run by a shadow state that replaced key officials with crooks. Ntombi spent a year in agony as she could not receive post-operative treatment after surgery on her spine. Eventually, once the state capture tide was on the turn, an honest, capable general was put in charge of the veteran system, and he sorted out Ntombi's case and those of many others.

Recently, three years after her retirement, something happened that brought all this back to us. I was driving through a military area and suddenly Ntombi leant over and honked the horn. She screamed, "Temba, wake up! I swerved and nearly drove into a ditch. Ntombi pointed to a cross by the side of the road, strewn with flowers. She explained, "That is where Temba was killed. I wanted to greet him and wake his spirit up." I put my shaking ands back on the steering wheel.

Temba (not his real name) was a competent, tough colonel from a rural area, with whom Ntombi had famous battles when she reported to him. He was a bully but highly efficient, and they both hated fraud and corruption. One day a vehicle suddenly drove off the road and killed him when he was out jogging. In my view, this appears to be a suspicious accident, especially as the driver of the commercial vehicle ran away and could not be found.

Some time later, I spotted a news report about the arrest of six members of logistics and procurement units in the defence force. The carpet of extreme corruption that had covered the country during state capture was being rolled back a little, like rotten turf, and some green shoots were appearing among the weeds of patronage and theft.

We were on our way to the military hospital, so Ntombi could get checked by her surgeon. He was a gruff Afrikaner for whom she had the greatest respect, not only because he had worked wonders when implanting her artificial knees, but because of the way he struggles tirelessly for the patients and organises his department. The South African Military Health Service uses scarce resources effectively by working as one team. It is an excellent example for any national health service when we finally get one.

I was at first upset by the sight of care being lavished on the elderly white soldiers and their families, when as young soldiers they had butchered people all over southern Africa. Then I was impressed by the professionalism and sympathy young black staff showed to them as well as to all their patients. Finally, I was deeply moved.

At the private system I go to, none of the specialists talk with each other. I have been literally ripped off: one surgeon had to save me from another one, who had stuck a titanium grommet quite unnecessarily in an eardrum. I am now more hearing-impaired and can never do any water sports again. I even have to wear an ear plug in the shower and swimming pool.

Ntombi has no problems with elderly whites being treated, and greeted several of them. "They are my pool buddies," she explained. She pointed at a building. "And that is where we used to go to the pool. Once or twice a week." The heated pool was donated by soldiers who raised the money in the 1980s. Like much else in the hospital, and the state in general, it fell into disuse through a connected web of wrong prioritisation, underfunding and theft of funds, often involving the Department of Public Works.

If I won the lottery or tripped over a diamond, the repair of the pool would be near the top of my list. Ntombi was many kilos lighter and in much less pain when she used to exercise with her Afrikaner pool buddies. Expert army physiotherapists taught them a combination of splashy Pilates, watery t'ai chi and wet yoga. She bonded closely with the group and they shared gossip, secrets and health tips. They still greet one another when they meet in a shop or parking lot.

"I love conservative Afrikaners more than anyone," she often says. "They always *maak 'n plan*, and they are very practical. With a lot of skills. And they don't bullshit." Ntombi promoted several Afrikaners despite bitter opposition from most of her ANC comrades. "I promoted the best workers. Those stereotyped people tried to stop me. What was best for the country? Who was being the real patriot?"

Several of the Afrikaners she recruited to her unit because of their skills were known racists who had used every opportunity to persecute black juniors. Without exception they become trusted colleagues and, in some cases, her friends.

Her first weapon was an unwavering commitment to putting the country first, and not friends or factions. Her second weapon was her being rooted in the family, including their families. Within a week she knew all their personal troubles and gave them advice and support. I would work closely with my staff for years without knowing the names of their wives and children.

Shortly after she retired, Ntombi was asked to speak at the funeral service of an Afrikaner staff member who, before he reported to her, would bin leftovers so that black cleaners working under him could not eat them. I accompanied her to a severe Calvinist church, packed with his family and congregation. They sat so still I was afraid to scratch under an itchy collar and had no idea why we were invited.

Philosophically a rationalist and a humanist, I value and respect any religion that gives me good spiritual guidance and emotions. I calmed down after remembering something that I found inspirational and beautifully ambiguous. It still gives me a profound feeling. It was written in Afrikaans on a wooden stand, on the desk of an elderly Afrikaner secretary who was always kind and helpful. "Be still. The Lord is listening."

At the funeral service Ntombi spoke well and with authority. I realised that the former colleague being buried was the person she mentioned as having once been a notorious racist. He became a friend she relied on to overcome problems at her work. Over the following months I listened to her stories carefully. I learned how she had helped many people with their lives by patiently ensuring they made better decisions regarding finances, marriage and much else.

When we visit the hospital for Ntombi to get medication or see a doctor, she always greets people she knows, from the corporal at the gate to the Surgeon General, who heads the military health service, if she bumps into him. In both cases she knows how their careers and family lives are progressing and how they are intertwined. Networking is another of her skills I have grossly underestimated and undervalued.

"That soldier over there", she told me, as we walked into the hospital, "now has a house because of me, like many others. I always told them to stop spending all their money. Save, and invest in bricks. You won't always live in an army house. And that one is still with his wife. I told him to stop fucking around."

Keep your Mother Teresa; I have Mother Ntombi, I told myself.

One night I asked Ntombi for advice as we were watching TV in bed. Our tendons were giving us pain, and it occurred to me that we could put time aside every day to exercise together. She could share the secrets of the pool with me.

Right then, the tendon of my right inner thigh began to cramp, and I asked what I should do. I forgot how strong she still was, and how direct. She grabbed my leg and threw it straight up into the air. It seemed she had forgotten it was attached to the rest of me. My hip joint complained bitterly. She then threw the leg sideways. "Then you pull back your foot, like so." The pain was intense but bearable.

The cramp went away and, until now, has not returned.

Nineteen

Surviving one another

We must learn to live together as brothers or perish together as fools.
– Martin Luther King, Jr., speech in St. Louis, 22 March 1964

I BELIEVE IN THE THREE FATES. One spins your life thread, another weaves it into the fabric of the universe, and the third snips it when your time is up. The cloth you leave behind can be ragged and threadbare or richly embroidered. Whether this is predetermined by the Big Bang or by something else is irrelevant. In terms of our thoughts, feelings and actions, we do what we do, and we all think and feel – on some level – that we can make decisions.

It was a few days into 2021, and the three of us who inhabit this house had to make decisions about how we plan to spin out whatever time each of us has left on earth. The moment I wrote the last sentence I realised I had borrowed it from Bertolt Brecht. My father told me that when in prison Bram Fischer had introduced him to a poem, "To Those Who Came After", which Bram said was his favourite.

Our forces were slight. Our goal
Lay far in the distance
Clearly visible, though I myself
Was unlikely to reach it.
So passed my time
Given to me on earth.

Bram died while a prisoner, but my father went into exile after his release and returned to play a part in the birth of the new South Africa. Both of them are now looking down on what is going on and shaking their heads sadly, from whatever place in Communist heaven some committee has sent them to.

I will soon turn seventy, Gogo eighty-five and Ntombi sixty-four. We try to be careful but we also take risks, and so Covid-19 and its variants may cut our threads at any time, though it is not likely to be at the same time.

It will take many years and a serious reform of the state and political and economic systems before we have a viable national health system. This implies that we will die in different places. I will probably die in a private hospital, Ntombi in a military hospital, and Gogo in a public hospital. Dying at the same time might make the news: "Three residents of one house died of Covid-related causes at exactly the same moment in three separate hospitals. The Statistician General says it creeps him out, as the probability is almost infinitely small."

Chances are, therefore, that whoever is left behind must organise things, such as finances and accommodation. Once again, I told myself that severally and collectively we need to do some planning and leave instructions for when we die. I suspect that few people leave such instructions. We ourselves have yet to do anything about it.

Ntombi organically builds the probability of threats and risk into the preparation and execution of her plans. She does it all within her head and keeps the project hidden from me until she decides on tactical grounds to reveal it. My approach is different. I use a computer to draw up a complex project plan with a section analysing risks, and then spend weeks talking about goals and strategies, and scaring myself out of taking action.

A department head I once worked for used a Xhosa expression to warn us against such tendencies, "A coward is always sharpening his spear". He explained that when the enemy arrives, you will have little left to fight with. I imagine a coward having a heavy shaft attached to a blade the size of a fingernail, instead of the broad stabbing spear invented by Shaka.

I remembered my vow that I would not leave Ntombi, until death do us part. That tired old phrase suddenly became terrible and real and, at the same time, wonderful. I vowed again to honour that decision, although there was a risk that she might kill me, as I will certainly continue to annoy her. Most experienced detectives have come across a case where a spouse, after fifty loving years, suddenly buries an axe in the back of the partner's head. The explanation given is often something like, "He sucked that tooth once too often."

As regards the possibility of being killed by Ntombi, a risk-mitigating factor is that, even though our personalities differ, we are similar in one important respect. Neither of us could live with someone who has no passions or vision or, worse, who does not strive to actualise them and generates negativity. In our bones, we are improvers, even if those bones are crumbling or attacked by gout. Going forward, our challenge was to find a way of surviving or, at least, enjoying our own passions and projects and those of our spouse.

Part of the answer, we both realised, was to agree on a final life project that we could both be passionate about. Our issues would not disappear, but we would have a better chance of resolving them while doing ourselves and others some good. What, I wondered, could each of us bring to such a project? Having pessimistic tendencies, I thought about two recent disasters that exposed my weaknesses.

For her last birthday I bought Ntombi a bread-making machine.

I explained that she would need it when her arthritis got worse and that I might also use it. A secret motive was to acquire the machine to challenge her mistrust of modernity and her hegemony over baking, for which she has a professional qualification.

I truly must have been mad, and Gogo tried to warn me using these carefully chosen English words: "I have a brain. I baked many times when working for that white family and at my home. That machine has no brain."

Ntombi's strategy was to pretend to give my bread-making project a chance, and to offer advice that is maddening. It felt like a know-it-all, irritating kind of help, but it was also useful. She helped me find or buy the ingredients for my first attempt at a loaf and told me about the trickiness of yeast.

"At that college in London where I did chef training, the lecturer was young and expected the students to make dough rise in the time of a lesson. I was the only one who managed, telling them that in my village we know it is a living thing and it must be as warm as my blood."

My first bread looked and tasted good, but it took me an entire day to set up and bake. The machine can take over four hours if you include a cooling-off period, as if it were a trade union dispute. My second attempt was quicker but flopped. Ntombi rolled up her sleeves, and produced three superb loaves in less than three hours. Every time I use the device, with whatever outcome, she bakes and does it better and faster by hand, while experimenting and improving.

For measuring salt, sugar and other dry ingredients Ntombi uses what my mother Sarah called in Yiddish the *nem* or "take" method. When we were newly married in London, she told me and Ntombi a story in which a mother-in-law defeats a young bride who relies on recipes. "You *nem* a handful of this and *nem* a handful of that," the bride was told.

The last time I used the machine, Ntombi moved against my project decisively. My loaf was tasty but sagged in the middle like a swaybacked horse. She used a scale to divide her handmade dough into two large and two small loaves, and explained that one of the baking tins was part of a set my mother brought into exile in the late 1960s. It was used to bake our wedding cake, thirty-five years ago. Ntombi is a romantic soul who forgets not.

This time it was different because Ntombi involved me in her making of the bread. Ntombi does not even measure the liquid. Water as warm as blood is poured as you knead the dough until it feels exactly right. I fetched, carried, and washed up, and kept the water warm by adding from a kettle I boiled each time.

I helped her to knead, pushing down with my fists, alongside small but powerful hands that were doing a rapid, rhythmic folding and refolding of the dough. After the baking and the cooling of the loaves, I bit into a slice, thick with farm-made butter and Ntombi's 2017 plum jam – a year when birds and bugs had left some fruit on our plum tree. They are farmers of a kind, after all, and wanted to harvest even more the following year when we relaxed our guard.

My bread-making project was effectively killed by Ntombi, leaving me mumbling about the future, when machines will have brains. Pathetically, I mentioned the use of artificial intelligence to crunch data from sensors that read the water temperature, gluten content, and barcodes on packets of yeast to know the species and the method of manufacture.

Ntombi had taught me the first lesson I needed to learn before we sat down and made our big retirement decisions. Do not rely on technology, and make sure you learn by doing.

The second lesson I had to learn was delivered two days later by a year-old Pekinese called Luna, belonging to our son Sipho and his partner Tiaan. Ntombi often cooks extra to attract Sipho and Tiaan to our house, as they must fetch the food unless they give a valid excuse. When they came to pick up two of the loaves of bread, they asked us if we could look after Luna the next day as it was their second anniversary. All three of us eagerly agreed, as we had looked after the puppy over Christmas, and she had wriggled her way into our hearts. "Luna, Luna," Gogo exclaimed, "very clever dog."

What surprised me was how bad I was at dealing with Luna and how good Ntombi and Gogo were. I was amazed by how much Ntombi enjoyed having the dog in the house. It had not been practicable to keep a dog when we were both working, as I refused to have a domestic worker. In addition, I secretly feared that Ntombi would beat the dog to death when it chewed on the furniture or to punish me. On a farm it would be different. She would regard a dog as an asset, valued somewhat more than me, although it would never come into the house.

I rushed around, feeding Luna, amusing her, and keeping her from eating something that would kill her, such as one of Ntombi's pills. I watched Ntombi and Gogo hobble around on their sticks or sit at the table, petting her and enjoying her attentions. I realised that this was a reversal of what had happened when Busi and Sipho were children. Ntombi and Gogo would do all the hard work, and I would come home, play with my kids, and read them bedtime stories.

Towards the end of our week with Luna, I overheard Ntombi laughing while on the phone with Sipho. "You must come and film your father with Luna. She frightens and chases him." This was a kick in the guts because it was true, and it was the second lesson I had to learn before we sat down to make decisions.

In Luna's big eyes, Ntombi was the alpha and omega, to be worshipped and obeyed. I was a resource that could not be trusted and who was at best feared, with a status on the same level as hers or lower. Next time they left Luna with us, I observed and reflected on my actions when interacting with the dog. I had to discover what gave Ntombi so much authority and what denied it to me.

Ntombi was dressed smartly, I suspected for the dog, and she had even put on a necklace. She looked relaxed, fresh and pretty, sitting at the head of the table. I concluded with a twinge of jealousy that having Luna around must be therapeutic. She bent down and greeted Luna in a calm, even tone, as befits a goddess. The dog did a dance of joy, even walking on two legs, and her tail wagged furiously.

I came forward to give Ntombi her good-morning kiss and Luna lunged at me, snarling and exposing needle-sharp teeth. Her eyebrows merged in a frown, her back arched, and her ears and tail were laid back.

Luna had changed from a cute gremlin to one that was given water after midnight and turned into an imp of Satan. She bit holes in my shoes and leapt in the air, possibly aiming at my groin. I retreated, protesting loudly, and she pursued me until I was two metres from Ntombi. She had already established similar perimeters around her bed, where she stored her toys and stolen treasures and her food and water bowls. If Ntombi and Gogo crossed these boundaries, they were met with a low growl, at most.

"Luna, sit," said Ntombi, and the dog went to her and lay down at her feet. "And that is what you should have done," said Ntombi, "You lose it ever time." Lose what? Any authority I may have had, of course.

I later found out that Ntombi and Gogo kept a secret store of fine crumbs on them that they let fall around Luna like manna from heaven. This was contrary to Sipho's strict instructions never to feed Luna other than at mealtimes and when rewarding her with treats.

When Luna threatened me, she was defending not only her goddess, but also her feeding ground. The crumbs might be tiny, but they generate hope of larger things, something many politicians and employers understand well. I gave Luna her meals and lots of treats but instead generated suspicion. My behaviour was unpredictable, and I must often stink of fear and aggression whatever my subjective feelings tell me. Perhaps, somewhere, they employ Pekes to supplement lie-detecting equipment.

Given my baking and dog-handling experiences, it was clear that in negotiating a retirement plan with Ntombi I could not bring technology or authority to the table. Looking back over my convoluted career, I realised that I best demonstrated leadership and management skills when working with small teams to deliver difficult projects. I decided that for our relationship to survive and thrive, Ntombi and I must agree to undertake a project that would require both of our skill sets and encompass what each of us is passionate about.

Ntombi fits her passions and plans into one word, "family", and she wants to be rooted in a society and a state that is committed to its interests. For that to happen, there must be clean, efficient and committed government.

I have a vision of a society and state that is founded on "inclusive development". It will be driven by a shared vision, empowered communities, networked business, and a professional public service. Our goals are different, but they overlap significantly. The problem we had to overcome is that we try to achieve our goals in very different ways and get very emotional.

One night Ntombi learned that her best friend and former colleague had been admitted to hospital with Covid-19 and had died shortly after. Ntombi had mentored the woman and worked closely with her over nine years. Her reaction to the death was to use her personal network to contact key people she felt needed to know, and to monitor what was happening with the family in case support or intervention was needed.

My advice to Ntombi was to stay clear of family matters. It was given without conviction and was ignored, as I knew it would be. When Ntombi relates to individuals, it is always together with their history and family, about which she never stops gathering information. This applies to a person she meets or else takes an interest in, such as Prince Harry. She ordered me to do research on him and she uses the information to comment on his behaviour, which she generally approves of.

I have little interest in families and the histories of their members, including my own, unless I can relate the information to a larger view of the world. My understanding changes as I absorb and integrate ideas, opinions and facts from arbitrary sources. It may be an item on the news or something I read or learn in a lift after chatting to a stranger.

In retirement, when issues and problems excite or concern me, I begin to construct models that I test against my information and analyses. I then research in a more focused way and engage with others through their work and also directly.

Those who like to keep things simple are driven mad by my approach, but over the longer term I sometimes add value. Examples could be drafting a better immigration policy, or a vision of Home Affairs as a modern department that can play a key role in the emerging digital world. My ten-year strategy was adopted as part of a White Paper supported by an Act, but its effective implementation must wait for elites that are development oriented rather than kleptocrats. Mind you, in the longer term we are all dead, as the economist John Maynard Keynes kept reminding the ideologists – sooner rather than later, given our local and global circumstances.

Without making a formal declaration, which after living together for thirty-five years is unnecessary, we have been carried to the same place by the forces that are shaping our lives. The project we have tacitly agreed on is to build a second home in the valley where Ntombi grew up. As a clan member she has rights to land there and has spoken with the chief, who welcomed the idea.

This is a strategy that many black rural migrants pursue after moving to urban areas, in order to remain part of their family and community. Ntombi could not make that decision because she was forced into exile and then spent twenty years following me around the country as I hopped from job to job.

I intend to become involved with the family and community on their terms while every day negotiating a way forward with Ntombi. The opportunity to learn isiZulu and about the culture and life of the community is a privilege; and Ntombi will guide me through the complexities of families and clans and people's relationships with one another. It is a perfect laboratory in which to test our different theories and strategies of development, and we will start by working with one or two people.

Of course, Ntombi has been plotting and planning this project for a decade, carefully grooming me at each step and revealing glimpses now and again. She uses peasant cunning and devious means to nudge me along. Money has been saved over more than a decade, and she mentioned a small budget for a cottage.

Over the past two years, the enclosed yard behind our kitchen had begun filling with piles of goods, in such a gradual fashion I did not spot what she was doing. She did not protest when I bought a new TV for the bedroom; and she wrapped the old one up and tucked it behind huge bags of rice, which I thought was our emergency food. We ended up with two old stoves wrapped and packed away in corners behind furniture I had always wanted to get rid of.

One of the stoves was for a family consisting of a mother whose child had been fathered by a young relative of Ntombi. Ntombi had spotted her as being smart, responsible and disciplined. I realised that it was not only me who was being groomed.

We started making trips to the valley where Ntombi grew up, and she made sure I met and got to know something about some local actors in her drama, witting and unwitting. Her phone calls to them increased from being monthly to weekly and then almost daily.

The masterstroke happened in the last half of 2021. Ntombi – without consulting me – gave our absent children absolute powers to effect changes to her beloved house. Busi, our daughter, drove the forty kilometres from Johannesburg to spend the weekend with Sipho and Tiaan, who live near us. They appeared on Saturday morning and informed us of the arrangements.

"We are going to Marie Kondo the fuck out of your lives and your house and declutter you," they announced, and started with the L-shaped room we use as a lounge and dining room, which leads down some stairs to a TV room. They then moved into our bathrooms. While a transformed house emerged, the piles grew even larger in the yard behind the kitchen as Ntombi selected extra items to go to certain people in Kwamteyi.

Two weeks later a young couple arrived from the valley, after an eight-hour drive with a van pulling a trailer. Sundry children, including one of their own, were in the van, brought along for their education. It was driven by a friend of theirs whose costs we helped cover. I also visited a corner shop to buy huge sloppy dagwood sandwiches and soft drinks for their journey back. As darkness fell, the van drove away into the sunset, pulling a mountain of goods that had been removed from our yard and packed onto the trailer. It would hopefully nourish one or two lives.

My pride in Ntombi and her works was boundless.

I began to do what I love best, researching and dreaming about doing something. Most nights Ntombi and I discussed options for building a house in the valley of her birth. There would be space for Gogo, but she made it clear she would visit but did not wish to live in a place where she had to work like a slave. We looked at designs I pulled off the web and adapted, and I researched composting toilets and the cost of water tanks.

What Ntombi loves best is action and getting things done. Tensions began to grow when discussing actually doing something – like deciding where and how to get builders. Covid restrictions stopped us from building, which would have put our partnership under pressure. We managed to cool things down and reach some agreements, as part of a longer process of finding better ways of making decisions.

In early February 2022, Ntombi informed me that she had a second Kwamteyi project, which needed to be completed in March. As I have mentioned, by the time Nomvula gave birth to Ntombi she was barely twenty and had already given birth to a girl, Thembalihle, who died after two months. Thembalihle's grave is on the hillside above the place where the family homestead used to be, and where the family still has two small houses. It was overgrown but strongly made of rounded rocks that were a beautiful rust brown. They were difficult to remove the ground, as roots of plants had gripped them and made them part of the fertile soil.

Ntombi wanted to replace the stones with a modern tombstone, for a reason. African graves are etched in the collective memory of the family, clan and community. She wanted the names of her dead siblings cut into solid granite, so they would not be forgotten and would be known to future generations. She was insistent that the birth and death of her younger brother Sifiso should also be recorded, and that the Carneson name must also be engraved on the black stone.

I discovered preparations for the ceremony were already advanced and a company contracted to provide a tent, chairs, a portable toilet and catering. She asked me to assist with ordering a tombstone and slab, with a message she would compose. I phoned my former secretary, Adelaide, whose advice I still seek from time to time, and who comes from KwaZulu-Natal. The company she recommended provided excellent and affordable service. I took with us a sound system and a battery to power it, plus a hand-held camera to record the event and the amplified speeches.

I booked the three of us into the Boer and Brit, a friendly guest house in Ladysmith. We drove down to complete preparations, and to investigate what building a cottage near the grave would entail. Busi and Sipho would join us the day before the unveiling, and I invited a young architect. He was a family friend and had sketched possible plans for a house. Ntombi contacted members of the scattered families and related clans, some of whom were willing and able to come.

The film of the event is available on TheGraspedImage.com website,[6] and it shows Ntombi at her most formidable, as well as the speeches of Abel, her Great Father, and two other relatives. There are subtitles in English. It gives a glimpse of the broad valley in which Kwamteyi is situated, and the hillside which Ntombi used to climb up from her homestead as a child, carrying food to secret ANC meetings held on top.

In her speech, if you are attentive, you will hear Ntombi mention that, while in exile, she dreamed that she flew back to Kwamteyi – much as I imagined flying over southern Africa in the first chapter of this book. Her dead siblings, Thembalihle and Sifiso, were holding her hands as they flew with her. I had never heard of this dream. Among many other things, she had kept the world of the spirits secret until she felt I was ready to hear about it.

Our project to build a cottage and live among the community

will unfold, and we will report our progress on the website, using photos and text. Among other obstacles, the council had allowed contractors to quarry away a large slice of the hill, exactly where Ntombi planned to build.

It has damaged the look, feel and ecology of the hill, and the council has probably broken national and local laws related to consultation and the environment. Attracting tourists to look around and have a cup of tea will be more difficult, among other development opportunities lost. They were not aware that dreams of building that house kept Ntombi's hopes alive across decades of exile and the struggle to give birth to a new South Africa.

Someone from another clan built a house on land adjacent to the quarry. At the Kwamteyi end of the valley there is no formal administration of land tenure, and rights mainly rest on historical occupancy by clans and evidence such as graves. We had to initiate an ongoing legal process to establish who had the right to use the land.

The Covid pandemic and the war in Ukraine are escalating the cost of building material and the diesel we would need to travel between our two homes. There will be other wars, climate change, more jobs lost, starvation and serious unrest, given our sick state and politics. We are rapidly ageing, with multiple aches and pains.

But Ntombi is Ntombi, and my love for her is still growing.

Postscript: The grasped image

I came across the following two photos too late for them to be included in the body of the book. The first shows my father's family making music. I pointed out to Ntombi that they had at least four different instruments among them. My uncle Antony, whom I had met when a child, was an expert player of the banjo until the use of lead in his plumbing business crippled his fingers. Ntombi and I visited his widow Hester and their daughter Anne, both of whom we liked very much.

There are two Carnesons I am especially proud of. One is my father, who had a scar on his face from being slashed with a razor when still in his teens. He had tried to stop a racist assault on a man of Indian origin while riding on a bus. He fearlessly fought racism and fascism throughout his life, as a soldier, journalist and political leader.

The other Carneson I got to know late in my life, and we communicate occasionally using the internet. He fought his way to the top of a highly competitive industry. Although relatively youthful, he heads up a branch of a corporation abroad. He is a successful capitalist, and has creativity and integrity of the kind we need in South Africa.

Ntombi insisted I include the other photo, which shows her and members of her extended family dressed in traditional attire. They are standing in a traditional homestead, with dwellings that many white South Africans call grass huts. The roof is actually made of reeds that are specially selected, cut and dried. The smoke of the fire built in the middle of the round dwelling cures the thatching and keeps out pests. Ntombi and her mother built such structures using mud bricks mixed with grass and then dried. Properly maintained, they can last for decades and keep the structures warm in winter and cool in summer.

To grasp this image, you need to know more. Ntombi and the other children are about to go to the annual Reed Dance. The homestead is part of the Swazi royal household, and they had been summoned by the King.

Notes

1 Bridget Hilton-Barber, *Student Comrade Prisoner Spy* (Cape Town: Penguin Random House South Africa, 2016).

2 Famously sung by thousands of women on 9 August 1956 when there was a mass march to Pretoria to protest against the extension of the hated pass laws to women. The translation from isiZulu is mine, as none of the translations I looked at seemed to capture the spirit or poetry of the verse sufficiently.

3 This was greatly helpful and I urge those caring for the dying to read it. Free downloads in English and several other languages are available at http://www.crossingthecreek.com/.

4 Mehmet Murat Ildan's quote is available on Goodreads: https://www.goodreads.com/quotes/9651665-if-we-can-give-to-urban-people-the-peasant-s-love. He actively promotes his quotes on Twitter and other social media.

5 For historical reasons it was known in the UK as a Public School, one of an exclusive group of private schools. The term private is used in the text to avoid confusion.

6 My website has the film of the unveiling ceremony: www.theGraspedImage.com in the blog section, which will continue to report on the ongoing story of John and Ntombi and add text and images.

JOHN'S ROOTS: BEFORE MEETING NTOMBI

My mother Sarah is sitting between her father Zelic (left) and mother Anna Rubin. I never met Zelic. Late 1920s, Johannesburg.

My father's parents, Antonio and Anne. I never met them, or even knew their names. 1950s, Pietermarizburg.

Fred and Sarah Carneson, WW2

Me, Ruth, Sarah, Granny Anna & friend

TOP LEFT *Ruth, Lynn and me, 1950s*

TOP RIGHT *Our guest house in Cape Town*

LEFT *Ruth, me, Sarah and Lynn. The last photo together in South Africa. We all left for London one by one in the 1960s and '70s and found ourselves in exile until 1993.*

In 1973, after Fred's release from prison and arrival in London, the Carnesons gathered in one place. Sarah is holding Lynn's child, Simon. Lynn is sitting by Charles, her first husband. Ruth is holding her child, Omri. Granny Anna Rubin was visiting London and is on the couch.

Taken in 1968, before Fred's release from prison. I was still at boarding school. Charles (on right) became Lynn's first husband.

Inhambane, Mozambique, 1978–79. I taught English at two schools.

The children's art reflects the bitter war of independence.

Some of my older Mozambican technical school students

A cultural festival. Mozambican culture was not recognised by the colonists.

SOMAFCO, Tanzania, where I taught from 1980–85. It was officially opened by the ANC in 1985.

NTOMBI'S ROOTS: BEFORE MEETING JOHN

Ntombi's maternal grandfather, Samuel Mbele, with two friends. Taken in the 1950s at Ekuphumuleni, meaning "place of rest". They were forcefully removed in the 1970s and the land was given to white farmers.

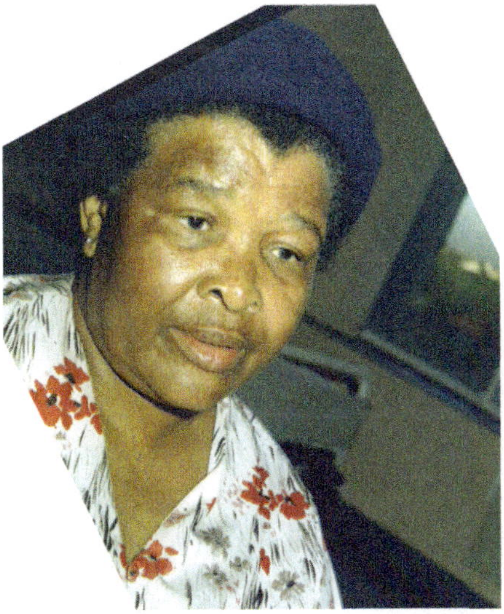

Ntombi's mother (left), Nomvula Mbele and her father Shoti Lukhele (right).

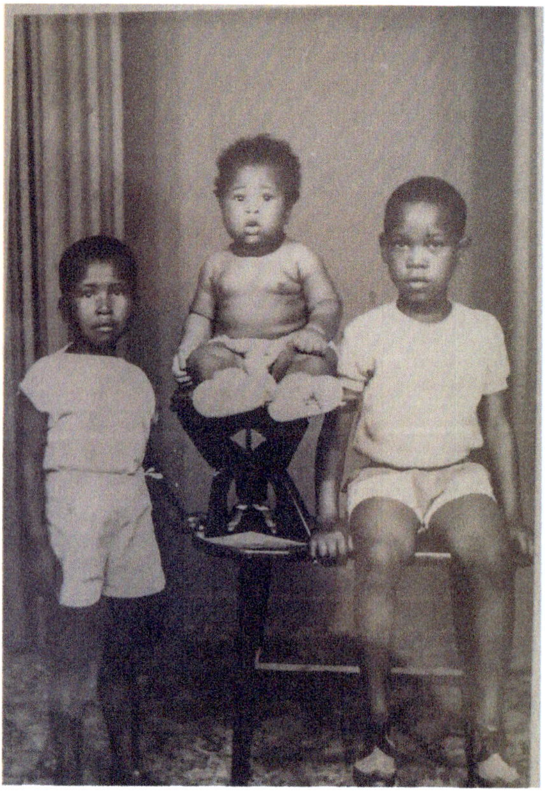

TOP *Ntombi's mother, Nomvula Mbele, was forced to find work with a white family when Shoti went into exile. She later divorced him.*

LEFT *Ntombi on the left, and her baby brother Khumbulani. On the right is Simangele Mbele. Both the Mbele and Lukhele families had members living in a township outside Ladysmith, who Ntombi visited and so met the Mbele children often.*

Mpiko Lukhele and HRH Princess Msalela Dlamini married. She looked after eight children, including Ntombi and her brother, Khumbulani.

Ntombi's Swazi family, from the left: Bongi (a clan member), Nonkululeko, Ntombikayise (Ntombi), Khumbulane, Manzolwandle, Tihlobisile, Mbongizozwa, Thabisile, Silingabuhle

Ntombi's paternal granny, maThabethe known as Beauty, visiting her in Swaziland after she had a serious car accident.

Ntombi at 21, after she graduated from junior high school in Swaziland

Ntombi studying institutional catering in Lusaka, Zambia.

JOHN AND NTOMBI IN EXILE

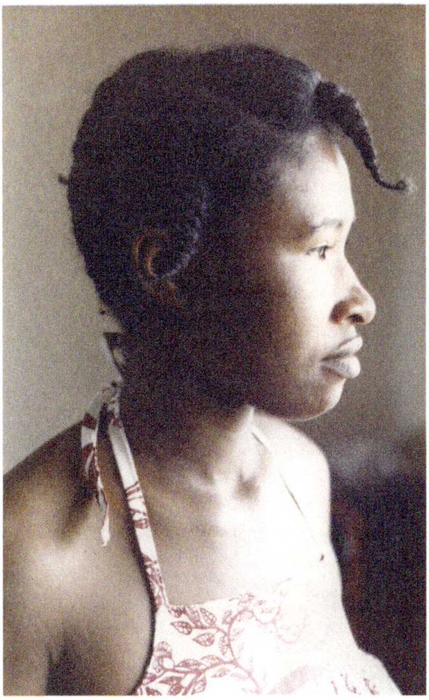

A portrait I took of Ntombi, Mazimbu, 1983

Our first child Busisiwe, meaning the blessed one, 1984

Busi was born in the hospital in Morogoro, the nearby town.

JOHN AND NTOMBI MARRIED IN LONDON

We got married in London in 1984. I had a fellowship at SOAS to write a history text book.

After the wedding party Ntombi returned to Mazimbu and I followed after completing the history book.

Fred and Sarah visited Mazimbu to be with Busi.

Fred and Sarah were shown the complex, including the farm and factories, the clinic, the nursery, library and primary and high schools.

JOHN AND NTOMBI IN EXILE IN LONDON

Ntombi and Busi with Fred and Sarah in London, 1986

On our way to holiday in Wales. Someone lent us their cottage.

People from SOMAFCO kept in touch when in London. Busi is still close friends with Naledi.

LEFT *Busi on her way home from a party.*

TOP RIGHT *The cake that Ntombi baked and decorated for Fred's 70th birthday.*

Busi and her Aunty Ruth.

Judith and husband Ndizingane from Swaziland visiting. He was studying in London.

JOHN AND NTOMBI IN EXILE IN SUNDERLAND

House-hunting in Sunderland.

We bought a cottage in Close St, near the city centre.

Kids popped in and out of each other's houses and played in the street.

The kids in the street celebrating Busi's birthday.

Busi started primary school, just around the corner.

Busi's primary school class.

She had a special friend, whose granny lived two houses down.

My research showed me how bright, collaborative and creative teachers and children can be.

Fred and Sarah drove up from London for a visit in 1990.

JOHN AND NTOMBI IN SOUTH AFRICA

Ntombi's mother Nomvula (Gogo) joined us before Sipho was born to live with us.

At first Busi saw baby Sipho as a serious rival...

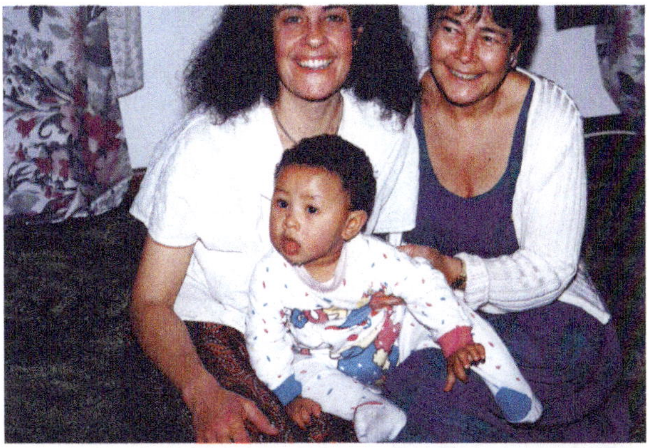

... especially when her Aunts Ruth and Lynn fussed over him.

Then they learned to get along, although not all the time.

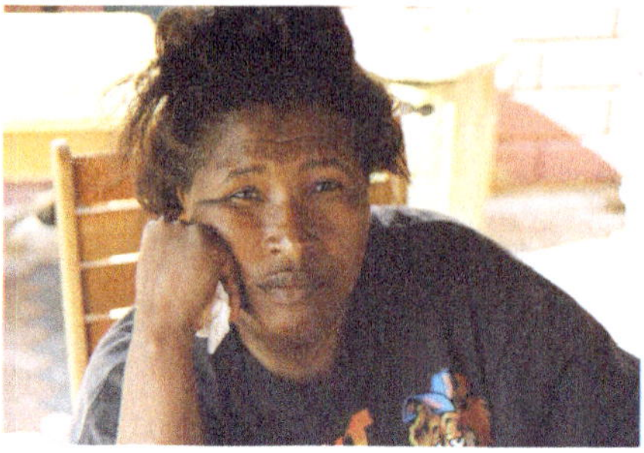

Ntombi had a lot to think about, including a tired workaholic husband. We both had low-paying jobs at the university. Her own family lived far away.

TOP LEFT, TOP RIGHT AND LEFT
As I hopped from job to job around South Africa, we kept in touch with our family and friends in Cape Town.

Our new South African passports allowed us to visit other countries. Ntombi is seen here deciding on which mask to buy in Venice, Italy.

Ntombi loved visiting food and craft markets. She is comparing beans with the stall-keeper in Hong Kong.

She buys a necklace in Morocco.

Ntombi fits a sari in India.

My cousin Wendy visited us from Australia. Some of the many relatives we began to connect with after returning form exile.

We began to meet with Ntombi's brother Khumbulani and his wife, Phiwe Mnisi.

Cousin Jasper (right) and his wife Rosie (left) visiting us from Italy, where Ntombi and I visited them.

I met Abel Mdluli, Ntombi's great father.

Visiting Swaziland, we met Nonkululeko, one of Ntombi's Swazi sisters.

In Ladysmith we met Nomvula's sisters Zamuzamu and Dokozi

We met Ntombi's Aunt Ngcane and MaZadso

It was Ntombi's first visit to her family in Ladysmith in more than 30 years.

Sarah Carneson's funeral in 2015 brought together many family members and friends. Busisiwe Lukhele came from Swaziland to represent Ntombi's family.

Me, Busi, Ntombi and Sipho Carneson, Simon McGregor (Lynn's son), Lynn and Ruth Carneson, Busisiwe Lukhele, Lionel Snell (Lynn's husband)

We were gathered at the spot where we had scattered my father Fred Carneson's ashes in the sea; and I had just scattered my mother's ashes.

We finally settled down to normal family life. Here we attend Sipho and Busi's graduations and Busi's 30th birthday party.

Busi's 30th birthday party

We celebrated the third anniversary of Sipho and his partner Tiaan. Their dog Luna adores Ntombi and (sometimes) tolerates me.

Throughout her years of exile, Ntombi dreamed about building a house near the grave of her dead sister Thembalihle, hidden by undergrowth. In March 2022, she erected a tombstone over the grave.

The unveiling ceremony brought the family together, overlooking Kwamteyi from the hillside where Ntombi was raised.

Printed by Amazon Italia Logistica S.r.l.
Torrazza Piemonte (TO), Italy

42155477R00125